THE KAISER'S SENATOR

Robert M. La Follette's Alleged Disloyalty During World War I

Arthur J. Amchan

D1715533

Amchan Publications
P. O. Box 3648
Alexandria, Virginia 22302

AMCHAN PUBLICATIONS
7010 Westbury Rd
McLean VA 22101
(703) 893 4717

Amchan Publications, P. O. Box 3648, Alexandria, Virginia 22302
© 1994 by Arthur J. Amchan
All rights reserved. Published 1994.
Printed in the United States of America.

Library of Congress Catalog Card Number: 93-91074
ISBN 0-9617132-3-2

Front Cover: "The Only Adequate Reward," by Rollin Kirby, *The New York World*, March 7, 1917, page 10. (This cartoon appeared after the successful filibuster organized by Senator La Follette against President Wilson's bill to arm American merchant ships to protect them from German submarines.)

Table of Contents

List of Illustrations/Photographs

". . . the man who obstructs a war in which his nation is engaged, no matter whether right or wrong, occupies no enviable place in history."

— Gen. Ulysses S. Grant, *Memoirs*.

CHAPTER 1

The Making Of An Iconoclast

In 1957, the United States Senate honored five of its outstanding deceased members by hanging their portraits in the Senate Reception Room. Senator John F. Kennedy of Massachusetts headed a committee charged with the responsibility for deciding on whom this honor should be bestowed. His committee polled 100 university history professors to choose the five greatest Senators. The top vote-getters were the twentieth-century progressive from Nebraska, George W. Norris, and Henry Clay of Kentucky with 58 votes. They were followed by Daniel Webster of Massachusetts (55 votes) and John C. Calhoun of South Carolina (30 votes). Tied with Calhoun was Robert M. La Follette, Sr., of Wisconsin (30 votes).

The Kennedy committee decided to honor the five with the exception of Norris, who was replaced by Robert Taft of Ohio, the conservative Republican leader who died four years previously.[1] While all five honorees

---

[1]Senator Kennedy explained that his committee believed they should select Norris or La Follette, but not both. *Congressional Record*, May 1, 1957, Vol. 103, pp. 6206-13. Though not explicitly stated, it is obvious that the Senators did not want the honors to go to two members whose views were so closely identified with modern liberalism. Conservatives, with some justification, may have felt that the choice of La Follette and Norris reflected the liberal bias of the academic community. In any event, Taft, the patron saint of post-New Deal conservatism, was selected instead of Norris.

Ironically, Senator Kennedy made a similar decision in picking the subjects for his prize-winning book *Profiles in Courage.* Kennedy devoted a chapter to Norris but omitted La Follette on the grounds that La Follette took his stand against American participation in World War I with the knowledge that his Wisconsin constituents supported his views. The future President was incorrect in concluding that La Follette's position was overwhelmingly popular in his home state.

9

were at times extremely controversial figures, only La Follette managed to evoke enough hostility to engender a serious effort to expel him from the Senate.

It is fairly safe to say that between February 1917, and November 1918, the period during which America debated and decided upon participation in the First World War, Robert M. La Follette was the most unpopular public official in the United States. How then did this man, widely denounced as a traitor, who Theodore Roosevelt stated on one occasion "ought to be hung," and on another said should be sent to Germany as a gift to the Kaiser[2], end up to be regarded one of the United States Senate's immortals?

Robert M. La Follette did not begin his political career as an iconoclast. Born in Primrose, Wisconsin, in 1855, La Follette began his political career as a prosecutor in Dane County, Wisconsin. The only evidence in his early life pointing to a career as one of the nation's principal nonconformists is La Follette's early antagonism to religious fundamentalism. He reacted bitterly to his step-father's constant assertions that anyone not baptized would languish in hell. La Follette's natural father had died unbaptized when Bob was an infant.

Nevertheless, in the three terms La Follette served as a Congressman between 1884 and 1890, there was never a hint that he was anything other than a traditional Republican, particularly on the issue of protective tariffs to aid American industry. Defeated for a fourth term, La Follette spent ten years practicing law until he took office as Governor of Wisconsin in 1900.

While Governor La Follette was indeed a different sort of politician than the man who had served in Congress ten years earlier, this was only true with regard to domestic issues. When midwestern farmers revolted against the economic and political control of their affairs by the railroads, banks, grain elevator operators, and other industrial interests, La Follette led their movement in Wisconsin. Joining forces with the urban factory

---

[2]Roosevelt to Henry Cabot Lodge, February 20, 1917, Morison, ed., *The Letters of Theodore Roosevelt* 8:1156-57; *The New York Times* (hereinafter *NYT*), October 1, 1917, 6:3.

workers, La Follette became the epitome of the new Progressive spirit running through the country.   Regulation of monopoly businesses; particularly the railroads, progressive taxation, and increased democratization of the political process through the direct primary, became the hallmark of La Follette's administration, and was often referred to as "the Wisconsin idea" when advocated in other states.

In foreign affairs, however, there was nothing that would lead one to predict La Follette's political near-martyrdom during World War I. The key issue of the Presidential election of 1900 was American imperialism and particularly the decision by President William McKinley, one of La Follette's closest friends during his Congressional days, to hold on to the Philippine Islands by force.   After liberating the Philippines from colonialism during the Spanish-American War, the President concluded that the Filipinos were not ready for self-government. The United States Army spent three years, 1899–1902, subjugating the Philippine nationalists. When William Jennings Bryan sought the Presidency in 1900 by galvanizing anti-imperialist sentiment in the United States, La Follette stood squarely with the Chief Executive.

During his three terms as Governor, La Follette acquired a national reputation as a reformer, and he built a potent political machine. In 1906, the Wisconsin legislature sent him to United States Senate, where he quickly alienated many of the "Old Guard" Republicans by refusing to accept the customary low profile expected of new members. Worse yet, during the critical battle over the Payne-Aldrich Tariff in 1908, he sided with the Democrats in vehemently demanding lower duties for foreign imports.

As the pre-eminent Republican progressive in Congress, La Follette was the first to seriously challenge President Taft's entitlement to renomination by the party in 1912. Angry at what they viewed as a lack of sympathy with forest conservation and excessive empathy for corporate development interests, many progressive Republicans, including ex-President Theodore Roosevelt, encouraged La Follette in his effort to wrest the nomination from Taft. However, when the Wisconsin Senator sought Roosevelt's endorsement of his candidacy, the former President remained noncommittal. As La Follette's efforts began to indicate widespread dissatisfaction with President Taft, TR, who may have always viewed La Follette as a stalking horse for his own candidacy, began to make plans to openly challenge his hand-picked successor in the White House.

Whether La Follette could ever have gained the Republican Presidential nomination remains problematical. However, whatever chance he may have had ended on February 2, 1912. The Senator and New Jersey Governor Woodrow Wilson appeared that evening as the featured speakers before the Periodical Publishers Association's annual banquet in Philadelphia. According to his older daughter and principal biographer, Fola La Follette,[3] the Senator arrived in Philadelphia by train from Washington at 11 p.m. suffering from indigestion due in part to the fact that his younger daughter, Mary, was scheduled for surgery the next day.

According to Fola, her father "took a drink of whisky, as he sometimes did prior to going on the platform fatigued."[4] Although Fola (whose husband was present) does not describe the Senator as being drunk, his performance certainly suggested as much. La Follette had planned to speak for 37 minutes from a prepared text but immediately got off on the wrong foot by antagonizing his audience. He attacked the newspapers and announced that he was using a prepared text because he was so often misquoted.

---

[3]The only full-length biography of Senator La Follette was started by his wife, Belle Case La Follette, and finished by his daughter, Fola. Mrs. La Follette had covered her husband's life only through 1910, when she died in 1931. Fola, who retained her maiden name after marriage to the playwright George Middleton, completed the biography which was published in 1953. Fola La Follette was an accomplished actress and was active in the women's suffrage movement and other feminist causes. She died in 1970 at the age of 87, after organizing the papers of her father and other members of her family for the Library of Congress. Obituary, *The Washington Post*, February 18, 1970, C4:1.

[4]Belle Case and Fola La Follette, *Robert Marion La Follette*, Vol. 1, p. 399-402.

The Wisconsin Senator then jumped back and forth from his text and rambled on sometimes incoherently for over two hours. Long before he finished, much of his audience had walked out. The next day newspapers reported La Follette's "collapse" at Philadelphia and hinted strongly that he was mentally unstable, an allegation that would plague him throughout the rest of his controversial career.

No sooner had La Follette stumbled, then ex-President Roosevelt announced his candidacy for the Republican Presidential nomination. La Follette supporters jumped to the Roosevelt bandwagon in large numbers. Among them was Senator George Norris of Nebraska, who in a few years would be La Follette's alter ego in the Congress and despised by TR almost as much as the Wisconsin Senator. Another defector was Wisconsin Congressman Irvine Lenroot, slowly emerging from La Follette's shadow to become one of his bitterest enemies.

After a brief hiatus in campaigning, La Follette was able to win the Republican Presidential primaries in his home state and in North Dakota. He flattered himself into believing that his 36 delegates might be critical to the outcome of the convention. However, the supporters of President Taft kept a firm grasp on the party machinery and easily renominated the Chief Executive. Theodore Roosevelt stalked off to accept the nomination of the Progressive Party and La Follette proceeded to sit out the presidential campaign. Although active in the campaigns for other offices on behalf of progressive Republican candidates, La Follette never said a word publicly as to which candidate he supported. It was widely assumed, however, that of the three major contenders, he preferred the Democratic candidate, Governor Woodrow Wilson of New Jersey.[5]

---

[5] Several people had commented on Wilson's solicitousness towards La Follette in Philadelphia after the latter's disastrous speech to the Periodical Publishers. Some observed wryly that Wilson had every reason to soothe La Follette's feelings, having just observed one of his primary competitors for the Presidency self-destruct.

13

Theodore Roosevelt's candidacy was by far the most successful third-party attempt to capture the White House. He finished second but managed to elect the first Democratic president in sixteen years. With approximately 40% of the vote, it is almost certain that Wilson could not have beaten either Taft or Roosevelt, if only one of them had been running.

After Wilson's inauguration as President on March 4, 1913, he consulted with La Follette as if the Senator were a Democrat. La Follette lobbied heavily for Wilson to appoint his close friend, the liberal Boston lawyer, Louis D. Brandeis, to his cabinet and was very disappointed when the President did not do so. Later when Wilson appointed Brandeis to the United States Supreme Court, La Follette was one of the leaders in the fight for his confirmation by the Senate, against a determined and nearly successful conservative opposition.

The Wisconsin Senator did more than just wait for leadership from Wilson. A month after the President assumed office, La Follette introduced his Seaman's Bill in the Senate. Previously American sailors had been completely at the mercy of their employers once they boarded a merchant ship. Anyone leaving a ship due to dissatisfaction with working conditions generally forfeited the entire salary due him. La Follette's bill entitled the sailor to one-half his earned wages whenever he left his employment and allowed him to leave his ship at any port where cargo was taken on or discharged. In response to the *Titanic* disaster the year before, the bill required an adequate number of lifeboats on larger ships and training of the crewmen in their use.[6]

Not only did Senator La Follette push his bill through the House and Senate, he was able to convince President Wilson to sign it into law after he and Andrew Furuseth, President of the Seaman's Union, made an emotional appeal to offset the concerted lobbying efforts by American

---

[6]A major reason for the large loss of life when the *Titanic* sunk in April, 1912, was the lack of lifeboats and the lack of experience of most of the crew members in lowering them.

shipping interests. One of the first attempts by the federal government to do something for the workingman, this legislation is generally known as the "La Follette Seaman's law."

The first indication of trouble between the Wisconsin Senator and President Wilson surfaced in April 1914, when the President ordered American forces to seize control of Vera Cruz, Mexico. After several Americans sailors had been detained by Mexican authorities and then almost immediately released, the navy insisted that the Mexicans salute our fleet. When they refused, Wilson, who despised the reigning Mexican dictator General Victoriano Huerta for murdering his predecessor, ordered the seizure of the Mexican port. In the ensuing struggle, several U. S. Marines were killed and others were wounded. Over one hundred Mexicans died due to Wilson's insistence on ceremony.

Immediately upon being informed of the spilling of American blood, a resolution was introduced in the Senate endorsing Wilson's use of force. The resolution passed 73 to 13. Those voting against the resolution were all Republicans and included arch-conservatives like Henry Cabot Lodge and Elihu Root, as well as progressives such as La Follette and George Norris. La Follette offered a substitute amendment for the resolution which disclaimed any long-range intentions on the part of the United States to exercise sovereignty or control over Mexican territory.[7]

---

[7]*NYT,* April 22, 1914.

"Fighting Bob" campaigning in Wisconsin, 1897 (Library of Congress)

The La Follette Family, 1910 (Bob, Sr., Belle, Fola, Bob, Jr., Phil, and Mary)

Senator Robert M. La Follette, 1911 (Library of Congress).

CHAPTER 2
War In Europe

On June 28, 1914, the Archduke Franz Ferdinand, nephew of the Emperor and heir to the throne of Austria-Hungary, and his wife were assassinated by Serbian nationalists in Sarajevo, the capital of the Austrian province of Bosnia. While nothing seemed to have less relevance to American national interests at the time, the assassination produced a chain of events that would send hundreds of thousands of American young men into battle in 1917 and again in 1941.

On July 23, 1914, after almost a month during which many believed that the crisis had passed, Austria-Hungary issued an ultimatum to Serbia. Included in the ultimatum were demands that Serbia stop the publication of anti-Austrian publications, dissolve anti-Austrian societies, and eliminate anti-Austrian books and instruction from Serbian schools. Less innocuous was a demand that Serbia fire any military or civilian official named by Austria. However, the demand most clearly inconsistent with Serbian sovereignty was one that Austrian officials be allowed to participate in the investigation of the Archduke's murder on Serbian soil. Austria-Hungary made this demand on the assumption that the small Slavic nation would be forced to reject it, thereby allowing Austria to wage a punitive war. The government of Imperial Germany gave its blessing to and encouraged the Austrian strategy. Kaiser Wilhelm II and his advisors deemed it necessary that Austria demonstrate to the Serbs and other ethnic groups within the empire that it was still a major European power.

Although Serbia agreed to most of the Austrian demands, it rejected the demand for an Austrian investigation inside Serbia, as the Austrians had expected. Czarist Russia, which considered itself the protector of the Slavs in the Balkans, took preliminary steps to mobilize its army. France, bound by alliance to Russia, assured the Czar of its support. On July 26, Sir Edward Grey, the English Foreign Minister, proposed that a conference be convened by the European powers to seek a solution to the crisis; while

19

France and Russia expressed interest, Germany and Austria declined. France then issued standby mobilization orders for its army.

Upon receiving the Serbian reply to its demands, Austria, on July 28, 1914, declared war. At this point, the first of many miscalculations that would send millions to their deaths and would upset the political stability of Europe for the rest of the twentieth century occurred. Austria-Hungary and Germany were convinced that Czarist Russia would not come to the defense of Serbia. The Russians had not intervened when Austria formally annexed Bosnia in 1908, and the conventional wisdom was that Russia's efforts to upgrade its military capabilities would not be sufficiently complete to contest Austrian action against Serbia for several years. Contrary to the Central Powers' calculations, Russia concluded that it could not ignore the Austrian attack and ordered the mobilization of its armed forces on July 30. Germany, on July 31, sent the Czar an ultimatum demanding that Russia rescind its mobilization order.

France, which formed its alliance with Russia in 1893, issued its general mobilization orders on August 1. Unreconciled to the loss of the French provinces of Alsace and Lorraine to Germany at the end of the Franco-Prussian War in 1871, republican France had thrown its lot in with the most reactionary regime in Europe. In some quarters, the alliance with Russia was deemed necessary to prevent further German expansion and in others was seen as the means through which France would regain its lost provinces.

The Czar refused to rescind his mobilization orders, and Germany declared war on Russia. Even though it had not declared war yet on France, Germany immediately put into motion its plan to attack the French. In 1905, the German Chief of Staff, General Alfred von Schlieffen devised a war plan predicated on Germany's need to counteract the Franco-Russian alliance. The von Schlieffen plan was based on the assumption that it would take Russia, given its vast distances and backwardness, far more time to effectively prepare for war than it would take France and Germany.

Von Schlieffen therefore decided upon the outbreak of the next war to hold the Russians at bay with a relatively small segment of his army. At the same time, a small number of German troops would defend against a French attack across the Franco-German border. The centerpiece of the plan was a huge German right wing which would smash through Belgium, get around the left (north) of the French army and achieve total victory in a matter of six to eight weeks.[1] Having defeated France, the Germans could then shift their forces to the east to fight the Russians.

One assumption of the von Schlieffen plan, that would turn out to be completely mistaken and would lead ultimately to the entry of the United States into the war, was a belief that England would not go to war if the Germans invaded Belgium or that, if it did, the war in the West would be over before English involvement mattered. However, the invasion of Belgium did bring England into the war. Without English involvement, the Germans may have been victorious, and without English participation on the side of France and Russia, America would certainly never have gone to war.

On August 2, German forces entered Luxembourg and the next day their cavalry entered Belgium. Although considerable opposition to supporting the French existed within the English cabinet, the opposition largely evaporated upon news of the invasion of Belgium. On August 4, Great Britain entered the war.

Undaunted, the German armies ripped through Belgium. On August 16 they captured the vital Belgian fortress of Liege and headed towards France. The right wing of the Kaiser's armies flanked the French and British forces and came within a hair of winning the war in just five weeks. However, French resistance stiffened in front of Paris (the battle of the Marne) and, by September 10, 1914, the Germans were forced to retreat to defensive positions.[2]

---

[1]The original plan also called for the German army to invade Holland, but was later modified.

[2]Professor James Stokesbury, at page 57 in his *Short History of World War I*, offers the following intriguing observation as to what might have been had the Germans been successful:

> It is perhaps legitimate to ask if Europe would not have been better off had the Schlieffen Plan worked. . . . [W]ould a German hegemony of Europe have been any worse than the subsequent course of the war,

The violation of Belgian neutrality, the heavy-handedness of the Germans in Belgium (exaggerated by English propaganda), the monopoly by England of war news available in the United States, and our common heritage and language all combined to dispose most Americans to favor the Allies (England, France, and Russia) from the outset. The German ambassador to Washington, Count Johann von Bernstorff, observed after the war was over:

> England proved victorious because the German Government did not realize that the War would be decided in Washington, while England was never in any doubt on this point and acted accordingly. Her victory was facilitated by the predominance of the English language. I fancy it would not be incorrect to say that the English language won the War. Thanks to its wide diffusion, the whole world saw, and still sees, through English spectacles.[3]

Nevertheless, sentiment to become involved in the war was not widespread even when Germany almost achieved victory over the French and crushed the Russians at the battle of Tannenburg in the first weeks of the war. Even ex-President Theodore Roosevelt, one of the first to advocate intervention on the part of the Allies, did not initially take this position. In an article appearing in the September 23, 1914, issue of *The Outlook*, Roosevelt expressed great sympathy for the Belgians. He warned that America had better start preparing militarily. It might be forced, like the Belgians, he warned, to defend itself in a conflict in which it had no direct interest. Nevertheless, TR, already aware of the German destruction of

---

with its millions of deaths, its influenza epidemic, its Bolshevik Revolution? [I]f the Schlieffen Plan had worked, Adolph Hitler might have remained a private in the Linz Regiment and Joseph Stalin a Georgian peasant.

[3] Bernstorff, *Memoirs*, p. 18.

the Belgian university city of Lovain, and its harsh measures against Belgian civilians, was not immediately convinced that German venality demanded action by the United States.

He observed that "when Russia took part it may well be argued that it was impossible for Germany not to come to the defense of Austria, and that disaster would surely have attended her arms had she not followed the course she actually did follow as regards her opponents on her western frontier." The ex-President continued by writing that "I wish it explicitly understood that I am not at this time passing judgment one way or another on Germany for what she did to Belgium." He then opined:

> It is certainly eminently desirable that we should remain entirely neutral, and nothing but urgent need would warrant breaking our neutrality and taking sides one way or the other. Our first duty is to hold ourselves ready to do whatever the changing circumstances demand in order to protect our own interests in the present and in the future.[4]

While the American government would not, in any event, have had any idea as to how to react to the startling events of August 1914, official bewilderment was heightened by the fact that President Wilson was virtually nonfunctional due to the rather sudden death of his first wife during the first week of the war. The firmest convictions with regard to the war were those of the Secretary of State, William Jennings Bryan, who wished to avoid American involvement at all costs.

It was not until the very early part of 1915 that the danger of America being drawn into the war became serious. Soon after the war started, England took advantage of its overwhelming naval superiority by effectively cutting the Germans off from virtually all trade with neutral countries, even in foodstuffs. This was a clear violation of America's neutral rights and drew angry protests from the State Department and

---

[4] Theodore Roosevelt, "The World War: Its Tragedies and Its Lessons," *The Outlook*, 108:169 at 170, 171, and 173 (September 23, 1914).

from President Wilson himself. Southern cotton interests were also annoyed with the British for interfering with their right to trade with the Germans.

Obviously England would gain tremendous advantage if it could monopolize the resources of the American economy for the Allies. Germany then resorted to only weapon it had capable of cancelling the British advantage, the submarine. On February 4, 1915, the Germans announced that effective February 18, they would consider the waters surrounding the British Isles a war zone. Thereafter, any ship flying the flag of any of the Allied powers would enter this area at its peril.

On February 9, 1915, Senator La Follette made his first public pronouncement on the war by introducing a resolution in the Senate directing the President to convey to all neutral nations the desirability of calling a conference to end the war and to mediate the disputes between the belligerents.[5] A few days later in speaking on behalf on his resolution, he warned that lack of agreement as to the rights of neutral countries was fraught with danger and added to the danger that unforeseen developments could draw the United States into the war.[6]

The "unforeseen" developments came much more rapidly than anyone expected. On March 28, 1915, an American citizen died in the sinking of the British ship *Falabra*. La Follette urged President Wilson to discourage American citizens from sailing on ships belonging to belligerent nations. The Wisconsin Senator noted that when domestic trouble developed abroad, as it had recently in Mexico, the United States had discouraged its citizens from traveling in the unstable foreign country and had generally taken the position that those who disregarded such warnings did so at their own peril. Why, he asked, should America take any different position with regard to American citizens who chose to endanger themselves by sailing on British ships?

---

[5]*NYT*, February 9, 1915, 3:3.

[6]*NYT*, February 13, 1915, 2:5.

24

President Wilson never considered such a course, and America almost ended up at war before even having a chance to think about it. On the first of May 1915, a notice from the Imperial German Embassy in Washington appeared in the New York newspapers. "Notice:" it said, "Travellers intending to embark on the Atlantic are reminded that a state of war exists. . . . [T]ravellers sailing in the war zone on the ships of Great Britain and her allies do so at their own risk."

On May 7, 1915, the British passenger liner *Lusitania* was torpedoed by a German submarine as it approached the British Isles. The torpedoes set off enormous explosions in the hull, which gave rise to a decades-long debate as to whether the liner was or was not carrying munitions. The *Lusitania* sank in the matter of 18 minutes, astonishingly quick in view of the fact that the smaller *Titanic* had stayed afloat for two and a half hours when it struck an iceberg three years earlier.

The death toll in the sinking of the British liner was 1,195; 128 of these victims were American citizens. Although some, particularly ex-President Roosevelt, wanted immediate action, others including former President Taft counseled caution. Within the administration, Secretary of State William Jennings Bryan pushed hard for a restrained response to Germany. Bryan argued that unless the United States was even-handed in protesting violations of our neutrality by the Allies as well as the Germans, it would forfeit its potential role as a mediator and become involved in a dispute in which we had no stake.

Wilson hesitated and on May 10, 1915, made a speech in which he declared that there is such a thing as "being too proud to fight." While those Americans who had qualms about going to war breathed a sigh of relief, Theodore Roosevelt bitterly assailed him for sacrificing the nation's honor out of cowardice. Wilson managed to alienate both the extreme advocates of war and the pacifists. Appalled by what he considered the overly harsh tone of Wilson's letters of protest to Berlin, Secretary of State Bryan resigned on June 8.[7]

---

[7]There is no doubt that Wilson was happy to see Bryan out of his cabinet. He was selected for this post solely because of his power in the Democratic party, having been its candidate for President in 1896, 1900, and 1908. He had no foreign

In Germany, a heated debate raged between Kaiser Wilhelm's civilian and military advisors as to how to respond to the United States. The civilians, led by Chancellor Theobald von Bethmann-Hollweg, advised caution. Although the Germans were uniformly angry about what they regarded America's weak response to violations of U.S. neutrality by Britain, ultimately the civilians prevailed. They convinced the Kaiser that Germany did not have enough submarines to make unrestricted submarine warfare effective and that continuation of this policy would bring America into the war--to Germany's disadvantage. On September 1, 1915, the German Ambassador in Washington, Count Johann von Bernstorff, informed the State Department that his country would not sink ocean liners without warning and without providing for the safety of non-combatants.

Although the acute war-threatening crisis between the United States and Germany appeared to be defused, events transpired in the United States which were very disturbing to those committed to keeping America out of the European war. In September, banker J.P. Morgan of New York concluded an agreement to loan $500 million to England and France. The government's tacit approval of the loan was a reversal of its position stated when the war began that loans to belligerent nations were inconsistent with U.S. neutrality. Bob La Follette denounced the loan in *La Follette's*, his monthly magazine.[8] He warned that by loaning money to the Allies, the U. S. was underwriting their military success and had ceased to be neutral.[9]

---

policy experience and generally was regarded as a buffoon by those who did have such experience. Although he deserves his reputation as a buffoon for his attack on the teaching of evolution in the 1920s, an argument can be made that Bryan served American interests in 1915 far better than the experts.

[8]Heavily subsidized, the magazine was never profitable during the Senator's lifetime, but was felt necessary by La Follette because the press, even in Wisconsin, was overwhelmingly hostile to him. After his death the magazine became *The Progressive*, under which title it exists to the present day.

[9]*NYT,* Sep. 20, 1915, 3:5.

With American money going to the Allies, British sympathizers attempted to foster enthusiasm for military service through the "preparedness movement." Among the leaders of this movement were ex-President Roosevelt and General Leonard Wood. Wood was a former Harvard medical student who made his name chasing Geronimo in northern Mexico in 1886 and then as TR's regimental commander in the Rough Riders during the Spanish-American War.[10] Wood, who had finished a term as Chief of Staff, remained Roosevelt's alter ego within the Army. "Preparedness" advocates pressured President Wilson to increase the size of the Army and Navy dramatically. General Wood initiated training camps for well-connected young businessmen and professionals designed to acquaint them with military service and proselytize them with his views regarding the need to prepare for war.[11]

Amid the mounting pressure on Wilson to begin preparations lest Germany force America into war, La Follette charged that the munitions industry was behind the entire movement.[12] The President, trying his best to straddle both camps, came up his own preparedness program. It alarmed the non-interventionists and failed to satisfy the friends of the Allies, but did succeed in satisfying the majority of Americans. As the war

---

[10]Wood was originally the colonel, regimental commander of the unit, officially the First United States Volunteer Cavalry, but was promoted to a brigade command after the regiment landed in Cuba. When Wood, one of Roosevelt's closest friends from his days as Assistant Navy Secretary, was promoted, Roosevelt took command of the Rough Riders and led them in their often inflated part in the American assault on San Juan Hill on July 1, 1898.

[11]The preparedness campaign was viewed by some of its promoters as the best course for keeping America out of the war. The less any belligerent (which to the people behind "preparedness" meant Germany) had to fear from the United States militarily, the less it needed to concern itself with America's neutral rights. However, the preparedness advocates never intended to force England to fully respect American rights, they wanted only to assure that Germany would be sufficiently intimidated that it would not interfere with U. S. trade with the Allies.

[12]*NYT,* Nov. 27, 1915, 4:3.

dragged on, the public, exposed only to British perspective of the war, was becoming increasingly pro-British and anti-German, but it was not ready to get involved in the European bloodbath.

In January 1916, midwestern isolationists attempted to counteract what they perceived as the drift towards war. Senator Thomas P. Gore of Oklahoma[13] introduced a resolution in the Senate calling on the government to refuse to issue passports for use on the ships of belligerent nations. A companion resolution was introduced in the House of Representatives. These resolutions affected only Great Britain because no other belligerent nation had ships sailing back and forth across the Atlantic. La Follette was an active supporter of the Gore resolution. The Wilson administration through intense lobbying was able to defeat the resolutions in both the House and Senate.

At about the same time, La Follette and six other senators spoke on behalf of a petition presented to the Senate calling for an embargo on arms sales to the belligerents. The Wisconsin Senator described the petition as "a cry from the common humanity of the country, which cannot find expression in the organized press, which has been appropriated by the powerful interests coining the honor of the country into money." *The New York Times*, vehemently pro-Ally, derisively observed that "the cry of common humanity which the Wisconsin Senator now hears was expressed at a convention of Pro-Germans at Sheboygan in October. . . ."[14]

While La Follette believed that allowing the American economy to become an appendage to the British war effort was inconsistent with neutrality, British sympathizers argued that an arms embargo was equally inconsistent with neutrality because, as a practical matter, it favored Germany. One hundred years earlier, President Jefferson had adopted a similar strategy to preserve American neutrality during the war between England and Napoleonic France. That experience did little to recommend the effectiveness of an embargo. Although England maintained naval superiority in 1807 and 1808, both warring nations had been contemptuous

---

[13]The grandfather of the writer Gore Vidal.

[14]*NYT*, Jan. 30, 1916, I 16:1.

of American shipping rights. Jefferson's attempt to withhold American trade from both belligerents failed to accomplish anything other than damage to the American economy. England and France managed to acquire their goods elsewhere or from American shippers who ingeniously evaded the embargo. Jefferson abandoned this strategy and ultimately America was pulled into war with England. The British, as in 1916, viewed their war in continental Europe as more important than abstract principles of international law, or American sensibilities.

La Follette was becoming increasingly wary of President Wilson's hedging on strict neutrality and concerned about the Chief Executive's obvious inclination to determine American foreign policy with as little input from Congress as possible. Nevertheless, when Mexican bandits led by Pancho Villa attacked Columbus, New Mexico, on March 9, 1916, killing 17 American citizens, La Follette was quick to express his support for the President's decision to send U.S. troops under General John J. Pershing into Mexico. The Senate adopted a resolution introduced by the Wisconsin Senator endorsing the invasion while extending assurances to the Mexican government that punishment of those who attacked Columbus was the sole objective of the expedition.[15]

No sooner had the American expedition into Mexico been launched then the country was back on the brink of war with Germany. On March 24, 1916, the French steamer *Sussex,* with 300 persons aboard, including a number of American citizens, was torpedoed in the English Channel with the loss of 80 lives. After a number of tense exchanges, the Germans backed down once again, promising not to sink such vessels without warning—unless the ship tried to escape or offered resistance. Yet at the end of the German note of capitulation sent on May 4 was a warning which should never have been very far from Woodrow Wilson's consciousness when he ran for re-election as the President who "kept us out of war":

> Neutrals cannot expect that Germany . . . shall for the sake of neutral interest restrict the use of an effective weapon if her enemy is permitted to continue to apply at will methods of

---

[15]*NYT,* March 18, 1916.

> warfare violating the rules of international law. . . . The
> German Government is confident that . . . [the United States]
> will now demand and insist that the British Government shall
> forthwith observe the rules . . . as they are laid down in the
> Notes presented by the Government of the United States to the
> British Government on December 28, 1914, and November 5,
> 1915.[16]

At about the time of the Mexican invasion, La Follette announced his candidacy for the Republican nomination for President in 1916. Although he won the North Dakota Republican presidential primary with token opposition, he managed to get only ten of the 26 Wisconsin delegates. The significance of his poor showing in the primary of his own state is that as early as the spring of 1916, it was evident that the electorate of Wisconsin was not solidly behind La Follette as he tried to correct America's tilt towards the Allies.

As the "peace candidate" at the Republican national convention in June, La Follette was only able to gain 25 votes in balloting for the presidential nomination. Supreme Court Justice Charles Evans Hughes was nominated to run against Wilson, with Theodore Roosevelt, who could have had the nomination had he not bolted the party in 1912, finishing a distant third.

The New York Times, a fairly good representative of prevailing public opinion on the East Coast could not contain its glee at La Follette's pathetic showing. It hopefully looked foward to his defeat in his re-election bid for his Senate seat. In castigating him for playing to the "hyphenates" (German-Americans and Irish-Americans hostile to Great Britain), the *Times* pleaded in an editorial entitled "The Badger Little Giant:"

> Wisconsin has one American Senator [Democrat Paul
> Hustings]. She needs another. . . . [La Follette's] vote on the
> Gore resolution should be in itself enough to beat him.

---

[16]Millis, *The Road to War*, p. 299.

Wisconsin should get rid at last of this noisy "reformer" who made "reform" his machine and office giver, the miscellaneous agitator, the fetter of American shipping. Let the Badgers give him back to the tents of Chautauqua and La Follette's Magazine. He has ceased to be even amusing.[17]

The Presidential campaign of 1916 certainly has to rank with one of the most disappointing in American history if one believes that purpose of our system of government is to give its citizens a choice on the critical issues of the day. The most overwhelming issue was whether the United States would get involved in war with Germany, and both candidates strived for perfect ambiguity as to what they would do with regard to the issue of war and peace if elected.

Although President Wilson would have preferred otherwise, his avoidance of war during his first term became the centerpiece of his re-election campaign. Unexpectedly, at the Democratic national convention, the keynote speech by former New York Governor Martin H. Glynn, emphasizing the fact that Wilson had "kept us out of war," was received so enthusiastically that the President's campaign managers decided to try to win the election on the abhorrence of war.

Wilson's hesitancy to emphasize this issue was due to the fact that he knew that he had avoided war only because the Germans had backed down when he demanded a cessation to their use of the submarine. Any reasonable person would have appreciated that the Germans, violators of Belgian neutrality, did not sacrifice submarine warfare because of their concern for international law, but only because the risks of unrestricted use of the submarine (American intervention on the part of the Allies) outweighed the benefits. A reasonable person would also have realized that events could at some point lead the Germans to conclude that the benefits of the submarine outweighed the danger of American intervention.

[17]*NYT*, July 1, 1916, 10:4.

While Wilson's hesitancy for a pacifist-oriented campaign shows an appreciation for these facts, what he didn't know was that the day of reckoning was only a few months away.[18]

Charles Evans Hughes had an even more difficult problem than the obviously misleading campaign that Wilson had to run to be re-elected. Hughes could not promise that he would intervene on the side of the Allies because the American public wasn't ready for it. On the other hand, he had to be careful about appearing too hesitant about the war for fear of offending a number of influential Republicans who thought America should have joined the Allies when the *Lusitania* was sunk. The depth of that feeling was best represented by Theodore Roosevelt's impassioned attack on Wilson at Cooper Union in New York a few days before the election:

> There should be shadows now at Shadow Lawn [Wilson's summer home in New Jersey]; the shadows of the men, women and children who have risen from the ooze of the ocean bottom and from graves in foreign lands; the shadows of the helpless whom Mr. Wilson did not dare protect lest he might have to face danger; the shadows of babies gasping pitifully as they sank under the waves; the shadows of women outraged and slain by bandits. . . . Those are the shadows proper for Shadow

---

[18]One of the most eloquent defenders of Wilson from the charge that his behavior before and after the war was hypocritical was the German Ambassador to Washington, Count von Bernstorff. Bernstorff observed:

> The fact that Mr. Wilson became our political enemy after the 31st of January, 1917, and that he consented to the Peace of Versailles, is no proof of the contention that before the 31st of January, 1917, he would have proved a similar failure as a peacemaker. The President's spiteful censure and treatment of us, both during the war and at Versailles , may be explained psychologically, by the fact that we rejected his efforts, as a mediator, and declared the U-boat war. Bernstorff, *My Three Years in America*, p. 369.

Lawn; the shadows of deeds that were never done; the shadows of lofty words that were followed by no action; the shadows of the tortured dead.[19]

Back in Wisconsin, Senator La Follette was challenged in the Republican senatorial primary by a conservative Congressman, M. G. Jeffries, who castigated the incumbent on domestic and foreign issues. In addition to La Follette's support for the Democratic tariff law, Jeffries made issues of the Senator's opposition to the preparedness movement and his call for an embargo on sales of weapons to the belligerents. Aided by campaign appearances on his behalf by Senator William E. Borah of Idaho and George W. Norris of Nebraska, La Follette won the primary with over 100,000 votes to Jeffries' 66,569.

The Democrats nominated William F. Wolfe, the son of German immigrants to run against La Follette in the general election. Wolfe accused the Senator of pandering to the "German" vote and also criticized him for his opposition to preparedness and his view that Americans should surrender the right to sail on belligerent ships. La Follette in his campaign was perfectly silent as to whether he preferred Wilson or Hughes in the White House. While his supporters asserted that the Senator was for Hughes, La Follette did not even mention the Republican candidate on the stump. Moreover, his praise of many of Wilson's domestic achievements could easily have been interpreted as an endorsement of Wilson.[20]

A few days before the election, La Follette gave a speech sharply criticizing Wilson, Taft, and Roosevelt, but sparing Hughes. Many La Follette supporters cited that as evidence that he preferred Hughes and suggested that he did not formally endorse the candidate only because he wished to be free to criticize his policies if he won.[21]

---

[19]Millis, *The Road to War*, p. 349.

[20]*NYT*, October 26, 1916, 6:1.

[21]*NYT*, October 26, 1916, 6:1; November 2, 1916, 6:3.

Despite, La Follette's obvious lack of enthusiasm, Hughes carried Wisconsin in the general election. After doing better than expected in the East, Hughes went to bed on election night with the understanding that he would be the next President of the United States. Surprisingly though, Wilson carried California, and narrowly won another term in the White House. As expected, La Follette was overwhelmingly re-elected to his Senate seat with approximately 251,100 votes compared to 135,100 for Wolfe. As we shall see, it is problematical whether he would have prevailed had he come up for re-election in 1918 rather than 1916.

In a signed editorial in the December 1916 issue of his magazine entitled "Jingoism Rebuked," La Follette argued that the election results were a mandate for Wilson to hold steady in his course to avoid war. Hughes' greatest liabilities, according to the Senator, were the support of Teddy Roosevelt, putting his campaign in the hands of Taft and other conservative Republicans, and "the appalling avalanche of money turned loose upon the country on the eve of the election in his behalf."[22]

It is doubtful that Wilson, basking in the warm glow of his electoral victory in December 1916, had any idea that the Germans were about to give him a few rather unpleasant surprises. At the beginning of the month, he wrote Berlin a note decrying the forced deportation of Belgian workers to Germany for labor in German munitions factories.[23] In mid-

---

[22]*NYT*, December 2, 1916, 4:3.

[23]*NYT*, December 2, 1916, page 1. Author's note: In researching this book, I was surprised to discover that the use of slave labor by Germany was not original with Hitler. As one who doubts the wisdom of our intervention in World War I, it is important to take note of the facts that support the argument that Imperial Germany was sufficiently venal and dangerous to warrant our entry into the war on the side of the Allies. On the other hand, impressed foreign workers during the First World War were not treated as badly as they were during the Second World War.

The German Ambassador to Washington, Count von Bernstorff, concluded that the deportation of Belgian workers by his government was a critical factor in leading America into World War I. President Wilson, the ambassador believes, delayed his peace mediation efforts because of the surge in anti-German sentiment in the United States at news of the deportations. Without this delay, Bernstorff

December, Germany asked the United States to initiate peace talks between it and the Allies. Secretary of State Lansing asked the belligerent nations to state their terms for ending the war and Germany refused. The Kaiser's alternative proposal, that a peace conference be convened in a neutral country, was rejected out-of-hand by the Allies.

Thus as the year 1917 began, it was apparent that despite the unprecedented carnage, neither side had given up on its hopes of defeating the other. In fact, two and a half years of war and the dimensions of the carnage only served to make any kind of compromise peace more difficult. The year 1916 had been marked by the battle of Verdun where 600,000 Frenchmen and Germans were killed or wounded while the battle lines of the two adversaries hardly moved at all.[24] To relieve the pressure on their French allies, the British launched an offensive near the Somme River on July 1, which managed to produce almost one million casualties before fizzling out in November. The political fallout from these battles was not a move towards peace. In England, France, and Germany, the men gaining power were not those looking for compromise, but those even more committed to achieving total victory over the enemy. In 1916, David Lloyd George, believed before the war to be a pacifist[25], became Prime Minister, largely due to the perception that he was more committed to victory than his predecessor, Herbert Henry Asquith. In France, power was shifting increasingly towards elderly Georges Clemenceau, whose staunch republicanism was overshadowed only by his unrelenting hatred for everything German. In late 1917, he become Prime Minister. To a nation

---

concluded, "the history of the world probably would have taken a different course. The American mediation would have anticipated [the German] peace offer and, therefore, would probably have succeeded because we could not then have reopened the unrestricted submarine campaign without letting the mediation run its course." Bernstorff, *My Three Years in America,* pp. 302-03.

[24]The German strategy at Verdun was simply to bleed white the less-populous French.

[25]Lloyd George first achieved notoriety for his opposition to English prosecution of the Boer War at the turn of the century.

whose army had barely survived widespread mutinies and whose population included many who had sickened of the conflict, Clemenceau promised, "[T]here will be neither treason nor half treason—only war. Nothing but war."[26] The cowed Chamber of Deputies gave the aging belligerent a landslide vote of confidence, 419 to 65. In the spring of 1918, when the Germans appeared again to be on the verge of a breakthrough on the Western front, Clemenceau reminded the Chamber of his program:

> I wage war! . . . And I shall continue to wage war until the last quarter of an hour!

To prove his point, he had the parliamentary immunity stripped from his pacifist political opponent, Joseph Caillaux, who was then prosecuted for treason and spent three years in jail.[27]

In Germany, by August 1916, the heroes of Germany's successful campaigns against the Russians, Field Marshal Paul von Hindenberg, and his chief of staff, General Erich Ludendorff, became virtual military dictators of their nation. So great was their prestige that they forced the Kaiser to follow their advice with threats of resignation on several occasions.

Whatever else World War I proves, it certainly shows that it is much easier to start a war, and even stay out of one, than stop one short of the total capitualation of one side or the other. Despite everything that came before it, each side in the Great War was convinced that one more offensive would do the trick. The failure of the French Nivelle offensive in the spring of 1917 almost destroyed that nation's capacity to wage war, but the army rallied behind General Petain and the civilians behind Clemenceau to continue the bloodletting. The Germans almost achieved victory in 1918, but the failure of their spring offensives, the miscalculation as to the impact of submarine warfare, and the arrival of millions of fresh American troops finally underminded the German will to continue fighting.

---

[26]Watt, *Dare Call It Treason*, pg. 282.

[27]Watt, *supra.*

Seeking to break the stalemate in Europe, President Wilson addressed the Senate on January 22, 1917. The President urged American participation in a league to enforce peace after the war ended. As to the current war, he warned that a peace based on victory by one side or the other could not endure. A permanent peace, he proclaimed, must be "peace without victory."[28] Although Senator La Follette was, probably for the last time, pleased with the President's message, reaction in England was not at all favorable. The British began to wonder about the assurances given to them by Ambassador Walter Hines Page as to the great sympathy Wilson had for the Allies.

---

[28]*NYT,* January 23, 1917, pages 1-2.

President Wilson and his cabinet. Secretary of State William Jennings Bryan is at the far right.

Kaiser Wilhelm II, Field Marshal von Hindenburg, and General Ludendorff

CHAPTER 3
America Enters the Fray

England's concern about America moving towards true neutrality was short-lived. Although Wilson didn't know it when he addressed the Senate on January 22, the Germans had already decided to reinstitute submarine warfare. On January 9, 1917, Chancellor Theobold Bethmann-Hollweg met with the Kaiser, von Hindenburg, and Ludendorff to discuss the U-Boats.[1] Heretofore, the Chancellor had been able to persuade the Kaiser to resist military demands for unleashing the submarine, but the context of the meeting and the enormous prestige of Bethmann's adversaries made the outcome of this meeting inevitable.

The armies of the Allies and the Central Powers were locked in a stalemate on the Western front and only the submarine, of which Germany had many more than two years earlier, presented any hope of breaking the deadlock. Hindenburg and Ludendorff reiterated the navy command's assurances that U-boat warfare would starve England into submission and force her to sue for peace before America could provide her any meaningful assistance. Although Bethmann-Hollweg remained skeptical of the navy's predictions, he had no alternative suggestions for concluding the war in a manner satisfactory to Germany.

---

[1]Since America's decision to intervene in World War I is often viewed through the prism of World War II, it is worth pointing out that Hindenburg, as the aging President of Germany, appointed Hitler as Chancellor in 1933 and that Ludendorff was the first of Hitler's prominent supporters. The latter was Hitler's primary accomplice in his attempt to overthrow the government of Bavaria and then march on Berlin in 1923 (the "Beer Hall Putsch"), served as a Nazi deputy in the Reichstag, and was Hitler's choice for President of Germany in 1925. Ludendorff had a falling out with Hitler—although they were kindred spirits with regard to the Jews. Ludendorff was also vehemently anti-Catholic, while Hitler's rise to power necessitated an accommodation with the church.

Even opponents of the U-Boat War, such as the Kaiser's Ambassador in Washington, Count Johnann von Bernstorff, recognized the political difficulties facing Bethmann-Hollweg and the Kaiser. After two and a half years of extreme hardship and appalling losses, public opinion in Germany would have been loathe to accept any peace terms, when a means of achieving victory, the submarine, remained largely untested. Had the German government waited for President Wilson's good offices to produce a compromise peace, the military and ultra-nationalists would never have forgiven it. Indeed, after 1918, when all military means of achieving victory or even a stalemate were exhausted, the right still blamed the civilian leadership for depriving the German army of its chance for victory in the field. It is no wonder that the Kaiser, with his Chancellor's acquiescence, decided to unleash the U-boat.

Ambassador Bernstorff received a cable from Berlin announcing that beginning February 1, 1917, all ships, including those of neutral nations, on their way to and from the Allied nations would be sunk.[2] The Ambassador had worked long and hard to keep America out of the war and believed the submarine campaign would surely bring the United States into the war and lead to Germany's defeat. He tried desperately to delay implementation of the decision—if for no other reason than to soften American reaction. However, by the time his cables reached Berlin, there was no inclination to reconsider. On the afternoon of January 31, 1917, von Bernstorff presented the German announcement to Secretary of State Lansing in Washington.

The German pronouncement did allow for free passage of one ship a week conspicuously marked. This "generosity" only inflamed American opinion in that its suggested that Americans and American ships could only sail at the sufferance of the Kaiser. There was a minority, however, that observed that America had tolerated English interference with America's right to ship nonmilitary articles to Germany for years.

---

[2]Previously German submarine warfare had been directed only at the ships of the Allied nations.

President Wilson's response to the German announcement was to ask the Senate to approve the breaking of diplomatic relations with Germany. With our national pride affronted, the Senate endorsed the President's request 78 to 5. The five who immediately dared to attempt to stop the rush towards war were La Follette, his alter-ego, Senator Asle Gronna, Progressive Republican from North Dakota, Senator John D. Works, a Progressive Republican from California, James K. Vardaman, Democrat of Mississippi, one of the most notorious race-baiters in our history, and William Kirby, Democrat of Arkansas. The most outspoken opponents of Wilson's policy were Vardaman and Works, who argued that Americans should be willing to waive their rights to travel in the war zone. Works, whose service as a teenager in the Tenth Indiana Volunteer Cavalry during the Civil War made his patriotism beyond reproach, dared to suggest that the Germans were justified in resorting to unrestricted submarine warfare due to military necessity.[3]

Once relations with Germany were severed, a clamor instantly arose to arm American merchant ships so that they could defend themselves against the Kaiser's submarines. On February 12, 1917, La Follette tried to beat Wilson to the punch by introducing a resolution to prevent the arming of American merchant vessels. He argued that equipping them with guns would make them more vulnerable to German attack rather than less so. The guns on the American merchantmen, he argued, would be ineffective against the subs, which fired before they could be seen. La Follette believed that arming these ships would likely increase the chances that the subs would shoot because it would be too dangerous for the U-boats to surface in the presence of armed merchantmen.

Following the sinking of the British liner *Laconia* with the loss of two American women, the President asked the Senate to approve the arming of American merchant ships and also for authority "to employ any other

---

[3]*NYT*, February 8, 1917, 1:1. Works obituary, *NYT,* June 27, 1928, 27:5. A less laudable aspect of Senator Works' career was his contribution to anti-Japanese hysteria in California. In 1915, he alleged that Japan had 30,000 military reservists in California and advocated stationing 200,000 permanent army reserve troops in the state to guard against Japanese attack.

instrumentalities or methods necessary to protect our ships and our people in their legitimate and peaceful pursuits on the seas."[4] This request for a blank check in dealing with German attacks was not completely the President's idea. His bitterest foe in the U. S. Senate, Henry Cabot Lodge, the ranking Republican on the Foreign Relations Committee, explained to his friend, ex-President Roosevelt, that he had added the expansive phrase to the administration's bill. Lodge, who was afraid that Wilson would not go to war, wrote Roosevelt:

> [I]f we did not [add the authority to use other instrumentalities] he would say that Congress wished to confine him to the protection of merchant ships. I have also come to the conclusion that we must force an extra session. Although I have no faith in Congress we should be safer with Congress here than we should be with Wilson alone for nine months. . . .[5]

Senator La Follette immediately decided to fight the President to the bitter end. Worse than the arming of the merchant ships was the President's request for unfettered discretion in responding to German threats. The Wisconsin Senator had become increasingly convinced that Wilson regarded the Senate's role in the conduct of American foreign policy with thinly veiled contempt. La Follette was as much concerned with checking the President's inclination to present the Senate with one fait accompli after another, as he was with the crisis of the instant.

Timing was all important to both La Follette and the President. Until amended in the 1930s, the Constitution provided that the life of each Congress and the term of the President ended at noon on March 4,

---

[4]*NYT*, February 28, 1917, page 1.

[5]*Selections from the Correspondence of Theodore Roosevelt and Henry Cabot Lodge*, vol. 2 p. 497 (letter of February 27, 1917).

following the election. Thus on February 27, 1917, when Wilson asked the Senate to consider legislation to arm American merchant ships, it had only six days to do so.

La Follette and other opponents of war with Germany believed the President was trying to rush the measure through without proper deliberation so that he would have the right to initiate war almost unilaterally until the next Congress convened its regular session in December 1917. La Follette wanted to delay Senate consideration of the bill until the 64th Congress expired to allow pacifist sentiment in the country to mobilize and to force Wilson to call a special session of the 65th Congress.

The great majority of the Senate, however, was more than willing to cede responsibility for war or peace to the President. The Senate Foreign Relations Committee voted in favor of the bill to allow the President to arm American merchant ships. When the Committee tried to expedite consideration of the bill, by the full Senate, La Follette objected.

By March 1, 1917, pacifists and opponents of war with Germany had begun to assemble in Washington to demonstrate and lobby the Congress. Most prominent in this group was the famed Chicago social reformer Jane Addams and former Secretary of State William Jennings Bryan. As Progressive Republicans began a filibuster in the Senate to force an extra session of Congress, the administration released a bombshell.

The government announced that it had obtained a copy of a telegram from the German Foreign Minister, Arthur Zimmermann, to the German Ambassador in Mexico City. The note, known in history as the "Zimmermann telegram," instructed the Ambassador to approach the Mexicans in the event that Germany went to war with the United States with the suggestion of an alliance between the two countries and possibly Japan. The telegram mentioned an incentive: the return to Mexico of territory taken by the United States during the Mexican War; Texas, New Mexico, and Arizona.

Although one can hardly blame the Germans for wanting to make American participation in the war other than risk-free, nothing could have done more than the Zimmermann telegram to push American public opinion towards war with Germany. As bad as inducing hostility by

45

Mexico was, the suggestion of involving the Japanese was worse. Although public opinion on the West Coast was less anti-German than on the East Coast, the hysterical fear and hatred of Orientals made many citizens of that region view the European conflict in a different light when they discovered that the Germans were willing to encourage Japanese belligerency towards the United States.

Although the Zimmermann note had the effect of seriously undercutting the opposition to American involvement in the war, there was still hope that it would prove to be a fraud, possibly a plant by British military intelligence. Even Senator Henry Cabot Lodge, a staunch friend of England, was cautious. He introduced a resolution calling on the President to send to the Senate all information that he had regarding German activities in Mexico. Senator La Follette supported the resolution but asked that it be amended to ask how long the United States Government had the Zimmermann telegram in its possession. Senator Works was also adamant about finding out whether Wilson was aware of the Zimmermann telegram when he asked the Senate for authority to arm the merchant ships. Obviously, Senate opponents of the President suspected that he had withheld this information so that he could release it with maximum affect to undercut anti-war sentiment.[6]

The hopes of American war opponents were dashed by Foreign Minister Zimmermann himself. One would think that a sophisticated public official such as Zimmermann would seize upon the opportunity to suggest that England was trying to trick America into war. That is not what he did; curiously, when asked about the telegram, he told the truth and admitted its authorship.

In Washington, although the chances of stopping American involvement in the war were decreasing every day, the hardcore opponents of the President were more determined than ever to force Wilson into calling an extra session of the next Congress. They received support from an unexpected quarter when Senator William J. Stone, Democrat of Missouri and Chairman of the Foreign Relations Committee, announced that he was opposed to the Armed Ship Bill and would yield management

---

[6]*NYT,* March 2, 1917, 2:2.

of the measure to the next ranking member, Gilbert Hitchcock of Nebraska. The decision by Stone was surprising because although he was known to personally oppose war with Germany and came from a state with a large German-American population (as did La Follette), heretofore he had shown complete willingness to do the President's bidding.

Hitchcock tried to expedite Wilson's armed ship proposal by suggesting that the Senate lay aside the bill pending before it and consider a similar measure already passed by the House. La Follette objected and debate continued. On March 3 and 4, 1917, as the clock moved towards the end of the 64th Congress, opponents of war spoke at length against the measure. Prominent among the speakers were George Norris of Nebraska, Stone, Vardaman, Works, and Albert Cummins of Iowa. The plan of this opposition was for La Follette to speak last with the longest and most comprehensive attack on the measure. Recognized as the foremost and most long-winded orator in the Senate, it was expected that La Follette would hold the Senate floor until the 64th Congress expired.

The record of the debate on the Armed Ship Bill in the Senate is most curious because of the constant interruptions to discuss other obviously less-pressing matters. However, one cannot help but be impressed with courage of the small band of opponents to the President's juggernaught and the clarity with which they expressed their views. On March 2, James K. Vardaman rose to plead for defeat of the bill. Heretofore Vardaman's great contribution to American political discourse had been repetitive lurid descriptions on the campaign trail of rapes allegedly committed by black men against white women. In his campaign for Governor of Mississippi, he became the nation's most vocal advocate of lynching as the preferred way of dealing with black crime.[7] However, few American politicians have so nobly committed political suicide as did Vardaman in 1917.

Vardaman announced his intention to vote against both the Army and Navy Appropriations Bills. He termed the plan for compulsory military training "un-American" and said he'd vote against these measures

---

[7]His primary biographer, William F. Holmes, contends that Vardaman as Governor actually took great pains to control lynch mobs, contrary to his incendiary campaign rhetoric. Holmes, *The White Chief: James Kimble Vardaman*, 1970.

on that basis alone. When he turned to the equities involved in the current crisis, the Mississippi Senator proclaimed:

> Great Britain has violated our rights upon the seas quite as often as Germany. Great Britain's unwarranted and flagrant violation of international law cost the cotton growers of the South during the years 1914 and 1915 more than $750,000,000. Was there any suggestion made to go to war with the Allies because of that crime against southern farmers? No. Can it possibly be less a crime to plunder the farmer than it is to inconvenience the munitions manufacturers?[8]

William Joel Stone, the errant chairman of the Senate Foreign Relations Committee, also took pains to match every German delict in complying with international law with a equally egregious violation by the Allies. He argued that England had been as contemptuous of Greek neutrality as the Germans had been of Belgian neutrality. He charged that the Russians had treated German civilians and prisoners with brutality equivalent to that exhibited by the Kaiser's army in regard to the Belgians. Finally, he argued that British interference with America's rights on the high seas was every bit as bad as that of Germany.

Stone conceded that there were many Americans "having no selfish interest to promote, whose undisciplined sympathies have made them partisans in the war." However, he placed the rush to war squarely on three groups; the munitions manufacturers, American shipping interests, and American bankers (particularly J. P. Morgan), who had invested in an allied victory.[9]

The Civil War veteran John Works took the floor the morning of March 4, his last day as a U.S. Senator. The issue, he said, was "whether the Government of the United States should go to war with a great nation

---

[8]*Congressional Record,* March 2, 1917, Vol. 54, part 5, 64th Cong., 2d Sess., p. 4778.

[9]*Congressional Record, supra.,* March 3, 1917, p. 4888.

for the purpose of protecting one or half a dozen American citizens who are traveling in this danger zone and who might very well keep out of it. . . ."[10]

Works argued vehemently that public sentiment in the United States was against war. The reason for this opposition was that:

> Germany is not moving against this country. She has not been guilty of any aggression against us. She has taken the lives of a few of our citizens, because they got in the way when she was prosecuting a war against another nation and fighting to preserve her existence. If the German Government should make aggressive warfare against the United States you would not need any exhortation in the Senate of the United States to arouse the patriotism of the American people. You would not be holding open your enlistment stations without getting any soldiers. . . .

Harkening back to his own youth, Works recalled that:

> I can remember the time, Mr. President, when my own good mother, without a murmur, gave up her boys to go to the Civil War. The mothers of today would make the same sacrifice under the same circumstances . . . but some patriotic mothers are protesting against their boys being sent to Germany or out upon the Ocean to battle with German ships for any such cause as has been presented up to the present moment; and, Mr. President, I join in that protest.[11]

The last opponent of the bill given the opportunity to address the floor was George W. Norris of Nebraska. Norris' destiny would make him one of the few members of Congress who would pass upon aiding England against the Kaiser, and a generation later against Hitler. His attitude in

[10]*Congressional Record, supra*, p. 4996.

[11]*Ibid.*, p. 4998.

the two situations was markedly different. In his address on March 4, 1917, Norris read a number of quotations from a scholarly work to the effect that a Congress, not subservient to the President, was essential to the American political system. His punch line to this part of his speech was that the work from which he quoted so liberally was authored by Professor Woodrow Wilson.

Norris then questioned the wisdom of Congress ceding its authority to this particular President. He recalled Wilson's exercise of his authority in 1914 when the government of the Mexican dictator, Huerta, had held a number of American seamen prisoner for an hour and a half:

> When Huerta found out that some American seamen had been arrested he immediately ordered their release and their return to their boat, and it was done. They were never confined in jail. They were only technically under arrest. . . .
>
> When that happened our Government that had never recognized Huerta demanded two things of Huerta. They said Huerta must apologize, and he must also salute the American flag; and because he did not salute the American flag the President sent our Army and Navy into Vera Cruz. We captured the city. We killed several hundred Mexicans who were innocent and were not to blame because the old pirate did not salute the flag. We lost 19 or 20 precious American lives in the attack. . . .
>
> Are we going to do something like that again? Are we going to get into trouble over some technicality like that?[12]

Strangely much of the time debating the bill was taken up by Senators, who at least publicly favored it. Obviously, if the objective of these men was to bring the bill to the floor of the Senate, they should have said as little as possible. There was no need to try to sway votes because

---

[12]*Ibid.*, p. 5009.

it was known that, if voted on, the measure would pass by a very large margin. Some of these speakers then obviously did not want to measure to pass, despite their public pronouncements to the contrary. Others, particularly Old Guard Republicans, while favoring the measure, shared the desire of war opponents for a special session of the 65th Congress—in lieu of giving Wilson a free hand during this critical period.

The administration got some measure of revenge when Senator Hitchcock ignored Senate rules and refused to recognize La Follette. In the waning hours of the 64th Congress, President Wilson arrived at the Capitol for his second inauguration. As he waited, the La Follette-led filibuster succeeded in preventing his Armed Ship Bill from coming before the Senate—although without the piece-de-resistance by the Wisconsin Senator.

The abuse heaped upon the successful filibusters is perhaps unparalleled in American history. *The New York Times* described their conduct as tantamount to treason.[13] Judge Alton B. Parker, the former Democratic Presidential candidate, who lost to Theodore Roosevelt in 1904, wrote the following salutation to William Jennings Bryan, his party's candidate in 1896, 1900, and 1908:

> If you and your friend Senator La Follette and your joint followers had gone to heaven three years ago Germany would not have attempted to drive the United States from the seas or to conspire with other nations to make war upon her, for we should have by now have been well prepared to defend ourselves, nor would you have occasion to sneak out of Washington upon the discovery of this German plot. While you can never undo the mischief you have planned, yet if you act quickly you may be able to persuade those now ambitious to become the Benedict Arnolds of Congress to end the shameful scene now being enacted.[14]

---

[13]*NYT,* March 5, 1917, 10:2.

[14]*NYT,* March 5, 1917, 2:2.

51

The most important salvo, however, came with a statement released by the President on the evening of his inauguration:

> [A]lthough as a matter of fact the nation and the representatives of the nation stand back of the Executive with unprecedented unanimity and spirit, the impression made abroad will, of course, be that it is not so and that other Governments may act as they please without fear that this Government can do anything at all. We cannot explain. The explanation is incredible. The Senate of the United States is the only legislative body in the world which cannot act when a majority is ready for action. A little group of willful men, representing no opinion but their own, have rendered the great Government of the United States helpless and contemptible."[15]

The next day Robert La Follette was hung in effigy by students at the University of Illinois in Champaign. In a similar vein, the trustees of Columbia University adopted a resolution to appoint a committee to investigate whether any faculty members were propounding doctrines which were subversive or otherwise unpatriotic. Meanwhile Wilson's response to his failure to get his Armed Ship Bill through the Senate was to ask his Attorney General to determine whether he could do so without congressional approval.[16]

Although La Follette's detractors loved to portray him as an unprincipled politician playing to the large number of German-American voters in his state, they were never very consistent about this accusation. *The New York Times* in lambasting the Senator, took pains to note that three weeks before the armed ship vote, the Wisconsin legislature passed a resolution expressing its loyalty to Wilson, that the faculty of the University of Wisconsin supported the President, and that La Follette had rejected the advice of friends to abandon his opposition to the bill when the

---

[15]*NYT*, March 5, 1917, 1:2.

[16]*NYT*, March 6, 1917, pages 1 and 2.

Zimmermann telegram became public.[17] Of course the *Times* attributed his stubbornness to pure vanity rather than principle.[18]

Expressions of support or admiration for La Follette in the nation's press were scant. A notable exception was an article in the *New York Evening Post* on March 6, 1917, by David Lawrence, who condemned the filibuster but gave La Follette and Norris credit for having the courage of their convictions.

> Two men alone really stand out as unquestionably guilty of the successful attempt to kill the Armed Neutrality Bill. These are Senators La Follette, of Wisconsin, and Norris, of Nebraska. The former objected constantly to a unanimous consent agreement for a vote. The other announced in a speech on Friday that he would "kill the bill" if he could. He sat alongside La Follette, and when the one did not offer obstruction the other would.

> There is a stoical courage in the way some of these men are acting in the face of nation-wide criticism. It is no pleasing thing to hear the outcries of "traitor" and to read widespread newspaper condemnation, especially from one's own state. Many of them realize that they can never be reelected. Those like Norris and La Follette who would have acted irrespective of the effect on their political fortunes are to be differentiated from others in the group whose opposition to the Armed

---

[17]*NYT,* March 7, 1917, 10:3.

[18]The *Milwaukee Journal,* the largest newspaper in Wisconsin, characterized the Senator as "unfaithful to his trust." This was no great surprise because the *Journal* and most of the Wisconsin press had been hostile to La Follette for years. In Cincinnati, a city with a large German-American population, the *Times-Star* characterized the Senator on March 5, 1917, as "La Follette and his little group of perverts."

Neutrality measure was not based on sound conviction, but on freakish views on the international situation or pro-German sympathies or other controlling expediencies of politics. . . .[19]

Another friend who went out his way to assure the Senator that he was not going to abandon him because he did not agree with La Follette's unpopular stand was Justice Louis D. Brandeis.

It didn't take President Wilson long to conclude that he didn't need congressional authorization to arm American merchant ships, and he announced that he intended to do so less than a week after his inauguration. The President also announced his intention to call a special session of the 65th Congress beginning April 16, 1917. The Senate, reeling from the criticism heaped upon it after the success of the La Follette filibuster, voted to change its rules to limit debate by a vote of 76 to 3. The dissenters were La Follette, Gronna, and Lawrence Sherman, Republican of Illinois, who said that although he intended to vote for the Armed Ship Bill, he deeply resented Wilson's attack on his Senate opponents.[20]

The special congressional session was moved up to April 2, and just before it convened Senator La Follette released a public statement detailing his reasons for opposing the Armed Ship Bill. *The New York Times* published his statement in full, albeit on page 7. La Follette said the bill was unconstitutional because it allowed the President to make war unilaterally and that it was useless in providing protection to our ships from German submarines. Why, he asked, should we wage war "for commercial advantages and fat profits beneficial to a limited number of our dollar-scarred patriots, for neutral rights which we surrendered to the belligerents on one side during the first three months of the European War?"

---

[19]*New York Evening Post,* March 6, 1917, 1:8-2:1; Belle C. and Fola La Follette, *Robert M. La Follette,* II, p. 636. Lawrence neglected to mention that many of those opposing the filibuster and rushing to war with Germany were also responding to the "controlling expediencies of politics."

[20]*NYT,* March 10, 1917, 1:1. The Senate terms of several opponents of the armed ship bill, most notably Works of California, had expired.

54

The clamor for war, he continued, was being "instigated by the money power and a subjugated press." He then questioned the President's motivation:

> The Armed Ship Bill meant war. In attempting to force it through in the last hours of the Sixty-Fourth Congress, the President made it plain that he desired to be left alone to exercise extraordinary and aristocratic power affecting the destiny of this country and the world from the Fourth of March to the assembling of the new Congress in the following December.

As to the efficacy of arming merchantmen, La Follette asked if was so easy to prevent submarine attacks, why hadn't the British navy been able to protect their vessels. He noted that the *Laconia* had been torpedoed twice without firing a shot.

Finally, he questioned the equity underlying the bill. If we were serious about reclaiming our neutral rights, La Follette suggested that we "assert those rights against Great Britain and her allies, as well as against Germany; insist on access to the Port of Bremen, as well as that of Liverpool, and hold all belligerents alike to strict accountability for unlawful interference with those rights."

The Senator charged that ever since November of 1914, "with feeble and ineffectual protest we submitted to [Britain] rifling our marts, prohibiting our commerce with the civilian population of Germany." Rather than go to war with Germany, La Follette suggested that "the United States might even now render the greatest service to itself, to humanity and the world, by calling a conference of neutral nations, whose object would be to enforce the rights of neutrals. The mere suggestion that food and other supplies would be withheld from both sides impartially would compel all belligerents to observe the principle of freedom of the seas."[21]

---

[21]*NYT*, April 2, 1917, 7:1.

At 8:35 on the evening of April 2, 1917, Woodrow Wilson strode to the podium to address a joint session of Congress. As the Senators filed into the chamber virtually each one carried an American flag or wore one is his lapel. The notable exceptions were La Follette of Wisconsin and Vardaman of Mississippi.

Although the air was full of excitement and almost everyone expected the President to ask for a declaration of war against the Germans, he had not divulged the nature of his address and maintained suspense for the perfect dramatic effect. After setting the stage with a recitation of recent events, Wilson stated, "[T]here is one choice we cannot make, we are incapable of making, we will not choose the path of submission."

With that sentence, the Chief Justice of the U.S. Supreme Court, Edward White, a Confederate army veteran from Louisiana, dropped the hat he was holding and with an expression of joy and thankfulness on his face brought his hands together high in the air with a "heartfelt bang." The House, Senate, and the galleries responded with a "roar like a storm."

The President continued and proclaimed that "the world must be made safe for democracy." When Wilson ended his address at 9:11, his audience was cheering wildly and waving their flags. However, not everyone cheered. A number of accounts took particular note that

> Senator Robert Marion La Follette, however, stood motionless with his arms folded tight and high on his chest, so that nobody could have an excuse for mistaking his attitude, and there he stood, chewing gum with a sardonic smile."[22]

The next day the war resolution was introduced in the Senate. Under the Senate rules, any member could prevent consideration of any bill for 24 hours, and La Follette immediately used his prerogative to delay war for another day. When chided by Senator Martin of Virginia as to the momentousness of the issue under consideration, La Follette snapped that he didn't need the lecture and recognized the seriousness of the issue as much as Martin.

---

[22]*NYT*, April 3, 1917, page 1 and 2:2.

On April 4, 1917, the Senate met for over 13 hours to debate the declaration of war. Seventeen members spoke in favor and five spoke in opposition. The first of the opponents to speak was Vardaman, digging his political grave a little deeper. Stone, the errant chairman of the Foreign Relations Committee was next. He dramatically proclaimed, "I shall vote against this mistake, to prevent which, God helping me, I would gladly lay down my life."[23]

Norris of Nebraska predicted that a stock market surge would follow the declaration of war. He charged that Congress was about to "put the dollar sign on the American flag" and was accused of treason by Democrats James Reed of Missouri (a rather lukewarm supporter of the war), Atlee Pomerene of Ohio, Ollie James of Kentucky, and John Sharp Williams of Mississippi.[24]

Senator Kirby of Arkansas stated that he was still opposed to the war but would vote for the war resolution because he believed war was inevitable. After a short speech by Gronna, La Follette then rose to begin a four-hour oration. He began by proclaiming that a Senator's duty is to vote according to his convictions, rather than stand behind the President regardless of whether he was right or wrong, as suggested by most of the nation's press.

The Wisconsin Senator then lashed out at Wilson for trying to silence him and questioning the motives of those who opposed him. Next he turned to the American press and observed, "The poor . . . who are the ones called upon to rot in the trenches have no organized power, have no press to voice their will upon this question of peace or war; but . . . at some time they will be heard."[25]

He ridiculed what he characterized as Wilson's misrepresentation of German promises. He quoted the German proclamation of May 4, 1916, promising to comply with international law [the "Sussex" pledge]. The Germans, he noted, warned the United States that:

---

[23]*Congressional Record,* April 4, 1917, Vol. 55, part 1, p. 210.

[24]*Congressional Record, supra,* pp. 214-218.

[25]*Congressional Record*, April 4, 1917, p. 226.

57

[N]eutrals can not expect that Germany, forced to fight for existence, shall for the sake of neutral interest, restrict the use of an effective weapon if her enemy is permitted to continue to apply at will methods of warfare violating the rules of international law.

La Follette observed that "[i]t must be perfectly apparent that the promise . . . was conditioned upon England's being brought to obedience of international law in her naval warfare. Since no one contends that England was brought to conduct her naval operations in accordance with international law . . . was it quite fair [for President Wilson] to lay before the country a statement which implies that Germany had made an unconditional promise which she has dishonorably violated?"[26]

To talk about fighting the German government and not the German people, as Wilson promised in his address, was meaningless said La Follette.

Sir, if we are to enter upon this war in the manner the President demands, let us throw pretense to the winds, let us be honest, let us admit that this is a ruthless war against not only Germany's army and navy but against her civilian population as well, and frankly state that the purpose of Germany's hereditary European enemies has become our purpose.[27]

If any part of La Follette's speech can be judged most prophetic, it would be this one. For in 1919 after the Kaiser had been forced to abdicate, President Wilson would join France and England in imposing draconian punishments upon the German people at Versailles.

---

[26]*Ibid.*, pp. 226-7.

[27]*Congressional Record*, April 4, 1917, p. 227.

Next the Senator ridiculed the President's pretension to a war for democracy.

> [T]he President proposes alliance with Great Britain, which, however liberty-loving its people, is a hereditary monarchy, with a hereditary ruler, with a hereditary House of Lords, with a hereditary landed system, with a limited and restricted suffrage for one class and multiplied suffrage for another, and with grinding industrial conditions for all the wageworkers. The President has not suggested that we make our support of Great Britain conditional to her granting home rule to Ireland, or Egypt, or India. . . .
>
> In the sense that this war is being forced upon our people without their knowing why and without their approval, and that wars are usually forced upon all peoples in the same way . . . but I venture to say that the response which the German people have made to the demands of this war shows it has a degree of popularity which the war upon which we are entering [does not] and never will have among our people. The espionage bills, the conscription bills, and other forcible military measures which we understand are being ground out of the war machine in this country is complete proof that those responsible for this war fear that it has no popular support and that armies sufficient to satisfy the demand of the entente allies can not be recruited by voluntary enlistments.[28]

To the argument that Germany's violations of international law were of a different character than those of England because the Germans killed American citizens, La Follette pointed out that the only reason that the English blockade had not taken American lives was that the United States had meekly submitted to England's violation of its rights. "If our ships had been sent into her forbidden high-sea war zone, as they have into the

---

[28]*Ibid.*, p. 228.

proscribed area Germany marked out . . . we would have had the same loss of life and property in the one case as in the other. . . . By suspending the rule...in Great Britain's case, we have been actively aiding her in starving the civil population of Germany."[29]

After a long discussion of Thomas Jefferson's efforts, as Washington's Secretary of State, to treat warring England and France even-handedly, La Follette closed his speech by offering the following alternatives to the declaration of war.

> One alternative is to admit our initial blunder to enforce our rights against Great Britain as we have enforced our rights against Germany; demand that both nations shall respect our neutral rights upon the high seas to the letter; and give notice that we will enforce those rights from that time forth against both belligerents and then live up to that notice.

> The other alternative is to withdraw our commerce from both. The mere suggestion that food supplies would be withheld from both sides impartially would compel belligerents to observe the principle of freedom of the seas for neutral commerce.[30]

As soon as La Follette had finished, Senator John Sharp Williams rose to angrily respond:

> [I]f immortality could be attained by verbal eternity, the Senator from Wisconsin would have approximated immortality. We have waited and have a speech from him that would have better become Herr Bethmann-Hollweg [the German Chancellor] of the German Parliament, than an American Senator. . . . I fully expected before he took his seat to hear him defend the invasion of Belgium—the most absolutely barbarous

---

[29]*Ibid.*, p. 233.

[30]*Ibid.*, p. 234.

act that ever took place in the history of any nation anywhere. I heard from him a speech which was pro-German, pretty nearly pro-Goth, pro-Vandal, which was anti-American President, anti-American Congress and anti-American people.[31]

Williams was followed by several other Senators speaking in favor of the declaration. Paul Hustings, La Follette's colleague from Wisconsin, a Democrat, attacked "hyphenates" (German-Americans and Irish-Americans supportive of Germany), urged the Senate to defer to the President, but avoided any personal attacks on La Follette.

The war resolution finally came to a vote. Eighty-two Senators voted in favor of the resolution and six voted against it. Three of the opponents were Progressive Republicans, La Follette, Norris and Gronna; the other three Democrats, Stone, Vardaman and Harry Lane of Oregon, who literally got up off his death bed to be counted against the war.[32]

Following the passage of the war resolution, La Follette was hung in effigy in Cleburne, Texas, and in Washington, D.C., (in Washington, the dummy labelled "La Follette" was accompanied by one labelled "Stone").

---

[31]*Ibid.,* p. 235.

[32]Lane died seven weeks later on May 24, 1917, after his detractors tried to initiate a recall petition (which didn't apply to U. S. Senators). Lane, during the armed ship debate, indicated an intention to kill Kentucky Senator Ollie James with a sharpened file, if James attempted to physically attack La Follette. One senses that Lane knew well that God was about to recall him and therefore didn't really care much what his political opponents in Oregon thought. William J. Stone also did not have long to bear his burden for opposing the war; he died of a stroke in April 1918.

Of the eight senators who were absent on the day of the war resolution, all were assumed to be in favor except possibly Senator Thomas P. Gore of Oklahoma. Gore, who introduced the resolution in 1916 to prohibit the travel of Americans on the ships of belligerent nations, never stated how he would have voted.

The *Boston Evening Transcript* said his opposition to the war was "the disloyal culmination of a career of selfish Ishmaelism. . . . Henceforth, he is the Man Without A Country."[33]

On April 5, the war resolution was brought before the House of Representatives. There opposition to the war was led by the Democratic majority leader, Claude Kitchen of North Carolina. The vote in the House was 373 for war and 50 against. Nine of the 11 Congressman from the Wisconsin delegation voted against the declaration. From Norris' Nebraska, the vote was split 3 to 3. Apart from Claude Kitchen, the negative vote that got the most attention was that of Jeannette Rankin of Montana, the first female member of Congress.[34]

Once the nation was at war, the administration turned its attention to the questions of mobilizing and protecting the country against German spies and Americans suspected of loyalty to the Kaiser. There certainly was legitimate concern with regard to espionage. The Germans had been active from the outset of the war in Europe in trying to mobilize German-American and Irish-American opinion to keep the United States out of the war. Two German military attaches were expelled from the country in 1915 for allegedly plotting industrial espionage against the United States. One of them, Captain Franz von Papen, would be destined to rise to the position of Chancellor of Germany in the early 1930s and then play the leading role in convincing the aging President von Hindenburg to name Adolph Hitler as Chancellor in January 1933.[35]

---

[33]Fola La Follette, *supra.*, pp. 666-67.

[34]*NYT,* April 6, 1917, p. 1 and April 7, 12:2.

[35]Von Papen entered the new government of January 30, 1933, as Vice-Chancellor and was supposed to be able to control and moderate Hitler. After a few years he outlived his usefulness to the Nazi regime and fell from favor. This setback worked to von Papen's longterm advantage. Tried as one of the approximately two dozen major war criminals by the victorious Allies at Nuremberg in 1946, he was one of three defendants to be acquitted.

The original espionage bill included a provision for press censorship through a board controlled by the President. Even some of the pro-Ally newspapers found this objectionable and it was dropped. La Follette, one of six Senators who voted against the final bill, was particularly concerned about the unfettered power it gave to the Postmaster General to prevent magazines and newspapers from being sent through the mails. As it turned out, Wilson's postmaster, Arthur Burleson, abused his power as much as it could have been abused.

The Espionage Act would ultimately be employed mostly against pacifists, socialists, and communists rather than German agents or sympathizers. Although nobody realized it at the time, the events that would make left-wing radicals so vulnerable to government suppression were beginning to unfold in the spring of 1917. In March, between the debate on the Armed Ship Bill and America's declaration of war against Germany, Russia's Czar Nicholas II abdicated, bringing the 300-year-old Romanov dynasty to an end.

While the Allies tried to bolster the new provisional government in order to maintain the Eastern front against the Germans, the Kaiser's government was sending the Russians a gift that would fundamentally change the course of history. In April, the Germans assisted the Russian revolutionary leader Vladimir I. Lenin in returning to his country from Switzerland in the hope that he would take Russia out of the war. This, the Germans hoped, would free masses of their troops for service in the West.

Senator George W. Norris of Nebraska, 1908

Mississippi's "White Chief," Senator James K. Vardaman

CHAPTER 4
The Draft

Prior to World War I, the United States had relied almost exclusively on volunteers to fight its wars. In its most recent experience, the brief 1898 war with Spain, the nation had raised far more volunteer troops than it needed.[1] The only concerted resort to conscription, during the middle of the Civil War had brought mixed results. It touched off large scale urban rioting in several northern cities and provided troops of questionable value to the Union army in the critical last stages of the war. The Civil War was primarily won by the re-enlisted volunteers, not draftees.[2]

At the end of April 1917, the Wilson administration introduced its draft bill in Congress and demanded that it be brought up for consideration almost immediately. La Follette questioned the urgency of the measure, citing protracted consideration of such a measure in Great Britain, which had depended on volunteers for the first two years of the war. Why, he asked, had Congress abandoned its usual practice of holding public hearings on a matter of such great magnitude. "Never," observed the

---

[1]Some of these volunteers found themselves fighting the Filipinos rather than the Spanish. However, after a relatively short time, the United States shifted to total dependence on its small regular army to crush the Philippine independence movement.

[2]Another critical source of manpower for the Union was the 180,000 black volunteers it began recruiting in 1863. Particularly in enabling Grant to extend his siege lines at Petersburg, these soldiers played a far more important role in the outcome of the war than white America has been willing to acknowledge until very recently.

Wisconsin Senator "in all my many years of experience in the House and in the Senate have I heard so much democracy preached and so little practiced as during the last few months."[3]

The Senator disputed that any emergency warranting conscription existed. He noted that there was absolutely no threat of invasion because the German fleet was bottled up in port by the British navy. The Germans hadn't even bothered to declare war on the United States after we declared war on them. La Follette pointed out the declaration of war did not necessarily require shipping American troops to Europe. Japan had made common cause with the Allied powers in 1914 and had shown no inclination to help the French and British on the Western front.

La Follette argued that the America's past practice of relying on volunteers had provided a superior army than reliance on a draft. He noted further that Canada and Australia had contributed significantly to the British war effort without conscription. Indeed, in Australia, conscription had been put to a national referendum and was defeated.

"The draft," La Follette proclaimed, "is the corollary of militarism and militarism spells death to democracy. No war can be successfully prosecuted that has not the spontaneous support of the men who do the fighting. . . ." He argued that never before had any country drafted soldiers to fight in foreign lands.[4]

From the historical record, La Follette cited statements made by Daniel Webster and Abraham Lincoln that he believed supported his position. He quoted the January 1916 congressional testimony of Nelson A. Miles, a Civil War general who also had been the Commanding General of the Army during the War with Spain. General Miles had told a House committee that he was absolutely opposed to conscription and recalled that at the time of the Gettysburg campaign many of the army's best troops had to be sent to New York and Philadelphia to suppress the draft riots.[5]

---

[3]*Congressional Record*, April 27, 1917, p. 1355.

[4]*Ibid.,* pp. 1357-8.

[5]*Ibid.,* pp. 1358-59.

La Follette proposed an amendment to the administration bill submitting the question of conscription to an advisory national referendum.

> If the friends of this bill are sure that it has the support of the people, they should be the first to agree to this amendment. If the principle of the bill has not the support of the people, it should be abandoned.[6]

The referendum, La Follette contended, could be conducted within 45 days through the Census Bureau and Post Office. In the interim, the country's military manpower needs would be filled through volunteer enlistments.

The Wisconsin legislator decried the lack of adequate protection for conscientious objectors. He prophetically observed that the bill did not "contain any provision to protect these people or any others from being singled out and made the special objects of military persecution under this law." Indeed, World War I was somewhat unique in the widespread mistreatment and outright torture of American conscientious objectors.[7]

La Follette closed his speech with an appeal to reconsider the steps already taken to bind the United States to the war aims of France and

---

[6]*Ibid.,* p. 1361.

[7]One of the worst offenders was General Leonard Wood, Theodore Roosevelt's friend. Wood apparently took out his frustration over being denied a combat command in Europe on the pacifists who had the misfortune to come within his realm.

Anyone who has the capacity to become indignant should read *Plowing My Own Furrow,* a book written in 1985 by 95-year-old Howard Moore, who refused induction during World War I. Among his recollections are being sentenced to 30 days solitary confinement and then being lashed to his cell door and beaten because he refused to stand at attention. This occurred at Ft. Leavenworth, the day after the Armistice (*Ibid.,* pp. 130-132). Several months later, at the whim of a particularly sadistic officer, the prisoners of conscience at Ft. Leavenworth were sprayed with high pressure fire hoses until one of them almost drowned (p. 143). Mr. Moore died in June 1993, at the age of 104.

England. He asked why the United States should not merely focus its attention on eliminating the menace posed by German submarines to American commerce instead of sending millions of soldiers to Europe to assist the Allies in bringing Germany to its knees.

The oration had, of course, no practical effect. La Follette's proposed amendment for a national referendum on conscription was supported by only three other Senators, Vardaman, Gronna, and Thomas Gore of Oklahoma. Among those voting against the measure was Senator Norris, a fact that annoyed Mrs. La Follette greatly.[8]

The administration's draft proposal passed the Senate 65 to 8, and the next day President Wilson announced his intention to send American troops overseas. Although everyone assumed he would do so, it would have been possible to wage only a naval war designed solely to keep the sea lanes to England open. Had we adopted such a war policy, as La Follette suggested, it may indeed have been possible to pursue our national interests independent of those of France and England in bringing the war to an end on terms less disruptive of international harmony.

In both the House and Senate, an inordinate amount of time was spent during the conscription debate discussing the offer of ex-President Roosevelt to raise and command a division of volunteers in France. France and England were very supportive of the idea; the symbolic value of a quick infusion of American troops led by the most well-known American in Europe would have been very valuable to Allied morale. President Wilson rejected the idea almost out of hand. He did have legitimate concerns as to military efficiency. He needed all the competent military professionals available to train and lead the torrent of conscripts entering military service and could not afford to have Theodore Roosevelt skim off the cream.

On the other hand, Wilson was not about to give a man, who had been castigating him for three years and calling him a coward, an opportunity to make political capital of the war. Roosevelt promised Wilson that if his offer to serve in the army was accepted, he would not return alive. However, the prospect of TR returning as the conquering

---

[8]Fola La Follette, *supra.,* p. 736.

hero and capturing the White House in 1920 provided the President with extra incentive to find reasons why a division commanded by Roosevelt would not be in the nation's best interests.[9]

After losing the fight over the draft,[10] Senator La Follette continued to fight the administration on the manner of financing the war. Wilson decided early to rely heavily on subscription to bond issues, which were done through highly publicized "Liberty Loan" drives. La Follette saw the reliance on bond issues as a scheme orchestrated by big business to avoid paying its share of the costs of the war. He urged reliance on progressive taxation, particularly on war profits and incomes. Although no more successful in this effort than in preventing the draft, La Follette had the support of 20 other senators in seeking to rely more on income taxes. William Borah of Idaho, Hiram Johnson of California, and his Wisconsin colleague, Democrat Paul Hustings, were among those supporting his proposed amendments to the War Revenue Act.[11]

---

[9]John Whiteclay Chambers in *To Raise an Army: The Draft Comes to Modern America* (1987) indicates a belief that Wilson's desire to avoid commissioning Theodore Roosevelt was the most critical factor in his decision to raise an army through conscription rather than by a volunteer system.

[10]A note regarding the military status of Senator La Follette's sons Robert M. La Follette, Jr., who succeeded him as Senator (1925-1946), and Philip, later three-time Governor of Wisconsin in the 1930s. In World War I, Phil joined the army ROTC program and became an officer, although he never went overseas. Robert Jr. developed a life-threatening bacterial infection and never served in the military.

Robert Sr. preferred that Phil join the Marines because Navy Secretary Josephus Daniels assured the Senator that he'd see to it that Phil did not suffer on account of being Bob La Follette's son. After the early end of his meteoric political career, Phil La Follette was a leader in the isolationist movement in the United States. However, he volunteered for military duty again in the Second World War and served on the staff of General Douglas MacArthur. The son of the most prominent anti-military politician in American history ended up being one of the primary supporters of General MacArthur's Presidential aspirations.

[11]*NYT,* August 24, 1917, 1:4.

La Follette was also determined not to let the patriotic aura surrounding the war obscure some of the unanswered questions regarding U. S. involvement. On August 11, 1917, he offered a resolution calling on the Allies to define the terms upon which they would be willing to make peace. The resolution also called for each ally of the United States to renounce the desire for territorial acquisition or indemnities from Germany. Finally, it called for the establishment of a fund subscribed to by all the belligerent nations, which would be used to restore devastated territory when the war ended.

A sharp reply to the La Follette resolution came from Senator Atlee Pomerene, a progressive Democrat from Ohio, soon to be La Follette's primary tormentor. Pomerene declared that the only support the La Follette resolution had was "from sympathizers of the Kaiser, slackers and [the] I.W.W."[12] Pomerene continued:

> The Kaiser would like Congress to pass such a resolution; it would give him hope that America was weakening and that the war would soon be over with America knuckling to Germany. Congress is nearly to a man with the President and will support him to the end of the war.

> There is no need to reiterate why America is in this War. Germany committed enough crimes against this country to make every American feel that peace cannot come until Germany, admitting her wrongdoing, asks for an end to the hostilities. It must be a repentant with which peace is made. . . .[13]

---

[12]The International Workers of the World, I. W. W., was a radical American labor organization, crushed by the government through use of the Espionage Act with the help of right-wing vigilante groups such as the American Legion.

[13]*NYT,* August 3, 1917, 2:8.

Pomerene's remarks, however, were mild compared to those made to the Union Club of New York by Elihu Root, President of the vehemently pro-ally National Security League,[14] and by the renegade socialist Charles Edward Russell upon their return from a mission to Russia to assist the Kerensky government in staying in the war. Intimating that war opponents were undermining the success of his mission, Root proclaimed:

> I feel that there are still some Americans who do not quite understand why we are fighting. If they did, these pro-German traitors who are selling [out] our country, who are endeavoring by opposition and obstruction in Congress and out of Congress to make what America does in preparation for the war so ineffective that when our young men go to the firing line, they will meet defeat—if the people all understand why they would rise and crush these traitors down to earth.

> There are men walking about the streets of this city tonight who ought to be taken out at sunrise tomorrow and shot for treason. . . . [T]hey are pretending to be for the country and they are lying every day and in every word.[15]

Russell, possibly to convince others of his patriotism, was no more restrained in his characterization of an unnamed American politician, although he was obviously referring to La Follette:

---

[14]Root was Roosevelt's Secretary of War and the architect of America's successful suppression of the Philippine independence movement at the turn of the century. He later served as Senator from New York.

[15]*NYT,* August 16, 1917, 1:1.

Disloyal American that disgraces the Congress of the United States. Traitor in disguise that has taken the oath of allegiance and goes to the Senate of the United States to do the dirty work of the Kaiser.[16]

A few weeks later, Russell, speaking to a gathering of pro-war labor union members in Minneapolis[17], markedly increased the vitriol of his rhetoric:

Riga [which had just fallen to the Germans on the Eastern front] was captured by United States Senators La Follette, Gronna, and Stone. When the Kaiser gives out the declaration of victory, he should give full credit to those men. They...are doing more to prolong the war and to slaughter American soldiers than all the soldiers of the Kaiser.

Foreshadowing the concerted effort to shut La Follette up and stifle all dissent, Russell proclaimed:

You people in Minneapolis don't have to sit down and watch a man like La Follette turn traitor. La Follette, Stone, and Gronna . . . have no more right in the United States Senate than Benedict Arnold has in heaven.[18]

---

[16]*Ibid.*

[17]The group, the American Alliance for Labor and Democracy, was headed by AFL chief Samuel Gompers, later one of La Follette's biggest admirers. Another giving a super-patriotic speech was the famed lawyer Clarence Darrow. Ironically, one of Darrow's biggest cases was defending the Socialist leader Eugene Debs, who was imprisoned for several years for expressing sympathy with draft resisters.

[18]*NYT*, September 7, 1917, 3:3.

4735

General John J. Pershing arrives in Paris

CHAPTER 5
The St. Paul Speech

On September 20, 1917, in this context of escalating attempts to stifle all dissent over American war policy, Senator La Follette travelled to St. Paul to address the Non-Partisan League, a progressive agrarian movement with a pacifist orientation. La Follette had expected to speak extemporaneously, although he had a few notes on the war revenue bill. A transcribed version of the speech shows that, in response to interruptions from his audience, La Follette turned his attention to the origins of the war itself:

> For my own part I was not in favor of BEGINNING the war.
> (Cheers and applause, greatly prolonged.)
> I don't mean to say that we hadn't suffered grievances. We had
> —A VOICE: Yes!
> . . . at the hands of Germany. SERIOUS grievances!
> —A VOICE: You bet!
> We had cause for complaint. They had interfered with the right of American citizens to travel on the high seas—on ships loaded with munitions for Great Britain.
> (Laughter, cheers and applause, long continued.)
> * * *
> I would not be understood as saying that we didn't have grievances. We did. And upon those grievances, which I regarded as insufficient—considering the amount involved and the rights involved, which was the right to ship munitions to Great Britain with American passengers on board to secure a safe transit.
> (Laughter and applause.)

77

We had a right, a technical right, to ship the munitions. And the Americans citizens have a technical right to ride on those vessels. I was not in favor of the RIDING on them,
(Laughter)
because it seemed to me that the CONSEQUENCES resulting from any destruction of life that might occur, would be so awful—   * * *
Let me state my position. Because a foreign vessel loaded with munitions of war, is technically foreign territory—
(Cheers and applause)
and an American citizen takes his own life in his own hands; just as much as he would if he were on the territory of France, and camped in the NEIGHBORHOOD OF AN ARSENAL!
(Cheers and applause)
. . . [I]t has sometimes occurred to me that the shippers of munitions of war, who were making enormous profits out of the business, invited and ENCOURAGED American citizens to ride on those ships, in order to give a sort of semblance of safety to the passage of their profiteering cargo aboard.[1]

La Follette then sharply criticized the administration and Congress for its unwillingness to finance the war by taxing those who were profiting from it. He concluded by pleading for open discussion of the country's war aims:

Abraham Lincoln, Daniel Webster, Charles Sumner, Henry Clay, and I might call the roll of all the great statesmen of that period, when the Mexican War was on, AFTER war had been declared, and they believed that the war was a wrongful war; they stood in places in Congress, and denounced the war. And Abraham Lincoln voted for a resolution to recall the American troops from Mexico.
(Cheers)

---

[1]Contemporaneous transcription by Norbert O'Leary, La Follette Family Papers, Library of Congress Manuscript Division.

And yet in these days of 1917, with the flags all about us commemorating liberty—constitutional liberty—we are inhibited from even DISCUSSING this war—from even SUGGESTING that there might be some way, with honor and credit to our government, to terminate it, and stop the awful slaughter, and the awful expense.
(Cheers, and waving of flags.)

Let me say in a word, if Abraham Lincoln was a patriot; if Daniel Webster was a patriot; if Clay and Webster and Lincoln, and ALL THE MEN OF THAT TIME UNDERSTOOD THE CONSTITUTION, and the rights of the people, YOU—the humblest one of you, HAVE THE RIGHT TO DISCUSS FREELY the question of whether this war might not be terminated WITH HONOR TO THE GOVERNMENT, and the AWFUL SLAUGHTER be discontinued.

I thank you for your patience.
(Cheers)[2]

Associated Press accounts of the speech quoted Senator La Follette as saying "We had no grievance [against Germany]"[3] rather than "I don't mean to say that we hadn't suffered grievances. We had—at the hands of Germany. SERIOUS grievances!" La Follette made much of this discrepancy in defending himself against charges of treason and sedition. In fairness to his critics, the inaccuracy of the news reports appears inconsequential. For although La Follette proclaimed that the United States had grievances against Germany, he proceeded to belittle those grievances.

---

[2]*Ibid.*

[3]*NYT,* September 22, 1917, 11:4.

The real issue concerning La Follette's speech is, whether once war has been declared, must a citizen, or even a member of Congress, stop criticizing the reasons for which the hostilities began. Must he or she stop all efforts to get the nation's course altered, for example, by getting Congress to change its mind about America's war aims, or replacing those public officials who voted for the war with others who will vote to end it. There is a fine line at best between statements which undermine a country's ability to wage war and those which legitimately can be made to revisit what to the speaker was an erroneous decision to wage war in the first place.

Theodore Roosevelt, in labelling La Follette the leader of the "neo-Copperheads"[4] of the present, challenged the Senator's historical precedents for unlimited debate on the war. It may be true that Congressman Lincoln believed he had a right to question the legitimacy of the Mexican War even after Congress had declared war on Mexico, but President Lincoln on numerous occasions attempted to stifle discussion of the legitimacy of his effort to crush secession with force. While the immediate emergency facing Lincoln was infinitely greater than that confronted in 1917, it is fair to ask why, if Lincoln could prevent Congressman Vallandigham from campaigning in Ohio against the war in 1863 and 1864, should La Follette have been allowed to undermine the nation's morale after U. S. entry into the First World War.

The St. Paul speech presented La Follette's enemies with their golden opportunity to silence him. Almost immediately after the speech, Governor Burnquist of Minnesota announced an official investigation of La Follette's allegedly disloyal statements.[5] At first, the Senator appeared undaunted. Two days after his appearance in St. Paul, he spoke to a gathering in Toledo, Ohio. He charged that his remarks in Minnesota were being misquoted and that the press was controlled by the financial interests of

---

[4]*NYT,* September 22, 1917, 2:4.

[5]*NYT,* September 22, 1917, 11:4.

80

the country and the "war party." He said that President Wilson had pressured Congress in declaring war and that the vote was in no way representative of American public opinion.[6]

La Follette's address in Toledo was his last speech made outside the Senate chambers during the war. The Senator quickly realized that his political survival was at stake and retreated to ride out the storm. Although his son's serious illness was a major factor in his relative inactivity between September 1917 and the end of the war fourteen months later, his opponents clearly had put him on the defensive.[7]

Theodore Roosevelt, speaking in Kansas City four days after La Follette's St. Paul speech proclaimed:

> If I were this minute a member of the United States Senate I would be ashamed to sit in that body until I found out some method of depriving Senator La Follette of his seat in that chamber which he now disgraces by his presence there. . . .
>
> Senator La Follette is at this moment loyally and efficiently serving one country—Germany.[8]

Roosevelt did agree with the Wisconsin Senator on one issue, however. He ridiculed the President's assertion that America was not fighting the German people, as well as their government. He agreed with

---

[6]*NYT,* September 24, 1917, 1:2.

[7]It's fair to note that La Follette fared better than opponents of the war in other countries. In Germany, Karl Liebnicht, a member of the Reichstag who was later killed in the Communist uprising of 1919, went to prison. Clemenceau in France vigorously prosecuted for treason those politicians who favored a peace of compromise.

[8]*NYT,* September 25, 1917, 2:2.

La Follette that the Germans had supported the Kaiser and concluded that they were therefore responsible for their country's crimes.[9]

On September 25, the Minnesota Public Safety Commission, of which Governor Burnquist was a member, adopted a resolution demanding the expulsion of Robert M. La Follette from the Senate. The resolution condemned the Senator as "a teacher of disloyalty and sedition, giving aid and comfort to our enemies and hindering the Government in the war. . . ."[10]

The next day speaking under the auspices of the National Security League in Chicago, ex-President Roosevelt called La Follette "the most sinister foe of democracy in this country" and charged that by implication the Senator had condoned the brutal murder of American men, women, and children on the high seas. Turning to pacifists generally, TR called them "old women of both sexes."[11]

In Racine, Wisconsin, on September 27, Roosevelt reminded his audience that Lincoln had sent the pro-Confederate Clement Vallandigham to the enemy lines and suggested that the new "copperheads" be treated the same way. At the end of his speech, the League of Wisconsin municipalities adopted a resolution calling for La Follette's expulsion from Congress.[12]

Moving on to St. Paul, TR lashed out again at La Follette and others who opposed the war but reserved most of his venom for those men claiming conscientious objector status. He said that the most vocal COs

---

[9]While Roosevelt attacked La Follette, his alter ego, General Wood was beginning a thinly veiled political attack on the way the war was being managed by Wilson and his Secretary of War, Newton D. Baker. Wood wanted to know why, almost six months after the declaration of war, no American troops were engaged on the Western front (they would not show up in large numbers until April 1918). Left unstated was the obvious fact that the Roosevelt Division would already have been fighting by this time—if Wilson had authorized it.

[10] *NYT,* September 26, 1917, 4:4.

[11]*NYT,* September 27, 1917, 5:1.

[12]*Ibid.,* Sept. 28, 1917, 10:8.

were unpaid agents of Germany and that the majority of the COs were either pro-German traitors or "slackers" [men too cowardly to do their patriotic duty].

Not to be outdone by the former Chief Executive, Congressman Thomas Heflin of Alabama[13] charged that certain members of Congress were in the pay of Germany. He called for an investigation of legislation introduced by La Follette and others to determine if there was evidence of financial support from the Kaiser's government. One anti-war member of Congress who didn't take kindly to these accusations, a Congressman Norton of North Dakota, initiated a wrestling match with Heflin the next time he saw him.[14]

The hysteria initiated by the La Follette's St. Paul speech reached a crescendo on September 29, 1917. Senator Frank B. Kellogg of Minnesota submitted a petition from the Minnesota Public Safety Commission asking the Senate to institute proceedings looking to the expulsion of Senator La Follette. The petition charged La Follette with teaching disloyalty and sedition and for giving aid and comfort to the enemy and hindering the government in the prosecution of the war. The resolution was referred to the Committee on Privileges and Elections, which was chaired by Atlee Pomerene, a progressive Wilson loyalist from Ohio. While the Committee included Kellogg, Ollie James of Kentucky and others personally hostile to La Follette, other members, including James K. Vardaman and Missouri's James Reed, were very sympathetic with his plight.

The New York Times waxed enthusiastically on the prospect of the demise of one of its least favorite political figures. In an editorial entitled "La Follette" appearing on October 1, 1917, the *Times* opined:

> Expulsion of this disloyal and dangerous member would be
> creditable to the Senate. To do so it would be necessary to have

---

[13]Congressman (later Senator) Heflin was the uncle of the current Senator from Alabama, Howell Heflin. Letter from Senator Howell Heflin to the author, September 10, 1992.

[14]*NYT,* Sept. 28, 1917, 1:6; Sept. 29, 1:4.

an impeachment trial. But the result could only be wholesome. It would have the approval of the whole country. Deprived of his position as Senator, the privileges of which he has so shamelessly abused, La Follette could no longer be dangerous. But as long as he remains in that body his influence throughout the country and beyond will be dangerous and his presence a dishonor to the Senate. He deserves expulsion.[15]

Bullies, particularly those of the reactionary stripe, were active elsewhere, including at Columbia University, where two faculty members were fired by the trustees for disseminating doctrines tending to encourage a spirit of disloyalty. Professor James Cattell of the psychology department was fired because he had written members of Congress in August 1917 urging them to prevent the shipping of draftees to Europe. Henry Wadsworth Longfellow Dana (the poet Longfellow's grandson) of the english department was fired for his association with a pacifist group.[16]

On October 6, 1917, Senator La Follette addressed the Senate for two hours with regard to the expulsion petition. He did not try to defend the St. Paul speech *per se* but rather attempted to cast the issue in terms of the broader principle of free speech. He declared:

> [I]t is not Members of Congress alone that the war party in this country has sought to intimidate. The mandate seems to have gone forth to the sovereign people of this country that they must be silent while those things are being done which most vitally concern their well-being. . . .
> * * *

---

[15]*NYT,* October 1, 1917, 12:1.

[16]*NYT,* October 2, 1917, 1:8. The noted historian Charles Beard resigned from the Columbia faculty a week later, citing as his reason the fact that the school had fallen into the hands of a small group of reactionaries. *Ibid.,* October 9, 1917, 1:3.

> I believe . . . that I am now touching upon the most important question in this country today—and this is the right of the citizens of this country and their representatives in Congress to discuss . . . every important phase of this war; its causes, the manner in which it should be conducted, and the terms upon which peace should be made.[17]

Much of La Follette's address was an extended citation to the speeches of Abraham Lincoln, Daniel Webster, and Charles Sumner opposing the Mexican War after American troops had become engaged. Sumner in Boston had attacked the war as immoral, and Representative Lincoln had specifically attacked President Polk for his lack of any clearly defined war aims. Webster, a year and a half after the war began had characterized it "most unnecessary" and "most unjustifiable."

In contrast, La Follette cited a speech by Treasury Secretary William G. McAdoo, President Wilson's son-in-law, declaring that every pacifist speech was traitorous. He then asserted that "the right of Lincoln, Webster, Clay, Sumner to oppose the Mexican War, criticize its conduct, advocate its conclusion on a just basis, is exactly the same right and privilege as that possessed by every Representative in Congress and by each and every American citizen . . . in respect to the war in which we are now engaged"[18]

La Follette concluded his remarks by reiterating his belief that it was Congress' duty to force the President to clarify the nation's war aims. Conceding that once in the war, America must see it through to the end, La Follette observed, "[I]t is not true that we must go through to the end to accomplish an undisclosed purpose or to reach an unknown goal." He argued that discussion and clarification of America's war aims would not strengthen Germany but weaken it. He suggested that the Germans would not be so uniformly committed to pursuing their government's policies with

---

[17]*Cong. Record*, October 6, 1917, p. 7878.

[18]*Ibid.*, p. 7881.

regard to America, if they were assured that America had no desire to dictate their form of government or render secure England's domination of the seas.[19]

This address brought rejoinders from several of La Follette's enemies, notably Republican Senators Albert Fall (the leading figure in the Teapot Dome scandal in the 1920s) and Frank B. Kellogg (later Secretary of State under Coolidge). Kellogg said the issue was not free speech but erroneous statements of fact by La Follette. Kellogg found most offensive the Wisconsin Senator's assertion that President Wilson had been warned by Secretary of State Bryan, before the *Lusitania* sailed, that the ship carried munitions in her hold. However, the nastiest retort came from Democrat Joseph T. Robinson of Arkansas, who said that if he felt as did La Follette, he would "apply to the Kaiser for a seat in the German Bundesrat."[20]

The New York Times in an editorial entitled "La Follette's Defense," disagreed with Senator Kellogg that La Follette's assertions concerning the *Lusitania's* cargo were important in deciding whether he should be allowed to stay in the Senate. The real issues the paper said were whether he made the statements in St. Paul that were attributed to him and, if so, whether he should be allowed to continue to make such statements in the Senate. The *Times* argued that free speech was not an issue in the La Follette matter; what was at issue was La Follette's duty as a member of the government to protect the lives of American soldiers. The paper described the Wisconsin Senator as "the man who has gone up and down the country uttering words for the encouragement of [our soldiers'] enemies and for the bewilderment and disheartenment of their Russian allies."[21]

Further evidence that the proceedings against La Follette were part of a broader effort by the government to stifle all dissent came from Postmaster General Albert Burleson. Burleson announced that all foreign newspapers would have to be licensed and that any that questioned the

---

[19]*Ibid.*, p. 7886.

[20]*NYT*, October 7, 1917, I, 1:5.

[21]*NYT*, October 9, 1917, 10:3.

motives of the United States Government or suggested that it was controlled by big business would be dealt with severely. Further, said Burleson, papers applying for licenses would be judged by their past utterances, and he already believed that most socialist papers would have difficulty obtaining a license on this basis.[22]

On October 11, 1917, La Follette formally replied to Pomerene, in his capacity as Chairman of the Committee on Privileges and Elections. He informed the Ohio Senator that he had received the transcript of his St. Paul speech and noted many differences between it and versions of the speech previously obtained by the committee. He noted first that he had not intended to discuss the *Lusitania* at all but had responded extemporaneously to interruptions from the audience.

The letter continued:

> I assume that the wholly false reports sent out by the press generally to the effect that I stated in various forms "We had no grievance" is receiving no credence from you, since that is contrary to the text of the speech you furnished me.

La Follette asked the Committee for permission to examine any witnesses the Committee might call if there were any factual issues with regard to what he said. He also requested the favor of presenting his own fact witnesses. He concluded, "[I]f the speech is to be otherwise questioned, or my right to make it considered by the Committee, then I respectfully request that I be so advised . . . and given the opportunity to be heard thereon in person and by counsel."[23]

Generally public figures and journalists joined in the attack on La Follette as sharks attack a wounded prey. Ex-President Taft, who himself had urged caution when the *Lusitania* was torpedoed, criticized the Senator for characterizing the right of American citizens to ride on British ships as a technical right. Taft asked, "Was the right of those

---

[22]*Ibid.,* October 10, 1917, 1:1.

[23]*NYT,* October 12, 1917, 7:2.

innocent . . . American men, women, and children, sent to their death
without warning on the *Lusitania,* to life and safety only a technical right?
It shocks one's deepest feelings to think that a Senator . . . could use words
of such an import."

Of course, La Follette had never said that the right of American
citizens to physical security was a technical right. He said the right of
such persons to travel on ships carrying the means by which England
would kill German soldiers was a technical right. President Taft also
seemed to forget that he, like La Follette, had not thought that the
Lusitania sinking was sufficient reason to go to war with Germany.

The New York Times, as if to prove that there was no limit to the
lengths it was willing to go to cast aspersions on the Wisconsin Senator,
published an article entitled, "The Psychology of La Follette," a pseudo-
scientific essay by Gertrude Atherton. Ms. Atherton alleged that La
Follette had never been the same since his mental collapse at the
Philadelphia Publishers meeting in 1912. Much of his conduct, she said,
could be attributed to his jealousy and bitterness towards Woodrow Wilson,
who had achieved all that La Follette had not. The article concluded with
the observation that "La Follette has a poisoned brain."[24]

While La Follette may indeed have been envious of President Wilson,
that could in no way explain his willingness to make himself the least
popular politician in the country in asking the nation to consider the war
and American policy from the German perspective. Further, why were
there not any assessments of the far-greater jealousy exhibited towards
Wilson by Theodore Roosevelt? Although motivated by sincerely held
views that Allied victory was essential to American national interests and
a belief that any war was good for the character of the nation, Roosevelt
harbored a hatred of Wilson that can only be described as pathological.

One Senator who publicly and forcefully defended La Follette was
Democrat J. Hamilton Lewis of Illinois. Shortly after the Committee on
Privileges and Elections began its deliberations over the petition from the
Minnesota Commission of Public Safety, Lewis was quoted as saying only
a handful of Senators favored the expulsion of their Wisconsin colleague.

---

[24]*NYT,* October 14, 1917, II, 2:7.

Lewis noted that a third of the population of Wisconsin was of German origin and another third was of Scandinavian origin, and he assumed that La Follette was merely voicing the opinions of his constituents.

Lewis recalled that La Follette had made the war in Europe an issue both in his primary campaign and in the general election in 1916. He had questioned the right of American citizens to travel on belligerent ships because he predicted that it would draw the rest of the country into war with Germany. Knowing his views, Lewis noted, the voters of Wisconsin had chosen La Follette to represent them in the Senate.

Senator Lewis, not known for his willingness to oppose the President, used his defense of La Follette's rights to raise, in a very thinly veiled manner, his own concerns about American policy. Lewis discussed the fact that the Scandinavian nations had territorial disputes with Imperial Russia and said these countries as well as Americans of Scandinavian origin had a right to know whether the United States had committed itself to Russian demands for Scandinavian territory. With approval, he stated that "[t]his is the question that Senator La Follette is voicing in their behalf."

The Illinois Senator also noted that there were issues regarding the fate of the German colonies in Africa[25] in the event of an Allied victory and the border disputes between Italy and Austria. While he declared that his views were different from those of his Wisconsin colleague on these matters, he was sure that La Follette represented the views of the majority of his constituents and that the Senate had no business in preventing these citizens from choosing La Follette from representing them in the Senate and giving expression to their opinions.[26]

Lewis was representative of a number of Senators who supported the administration publicly but shared La Follette's concerns about the uncharted waters into which Woodrow Wilson was steering the United

---

[25]Imperial Germany had four major African colonies: Togoland, Cameroon, German Southwest Africa, and German East Africa (the present Tanzania), all of which were taken by the victors at Versailles.

[26]*NYT*, October 14, 1917, 10:1.

States. Some of these, while not willing to defend La Follette publicly, cooperated in delaying final consideration of the expulsion petition. These legislators admired La Follette's willingness to bear the brunt of public disapproval for expressing reservations with American policy that they believed should be brought to the public's attention.

Meanwhile La Follette, responding to an invitation from Chairman Pomerene to appear before the Committee on Privileges and Elections on October 16, 1917, asked the Committee to specify as to what parts of his speech accuracy was an issue. Through his counsel, Gilbert Roe, a former law partner then practicing in New York, La Follette demanded the right to inspect any evidence questioning the accuracy of his speech and informed the Committee he would not appear before it until his demands were met.[27]

Receiving no reply to his requests, La Follette appeared before Pomerene's Committee on October 16, called its procedure "an insult," announced his unwillingness to participate, and stormed out of the hearing room.[28] Although buoyed by the support of his friends, the Senator was still receiving an unrelenting barrage of abuse. The New York City Republican Club unanimously adopted a resolution calling on the Senate to expel him, and the Wisconsin State and County Councils of Defense adopted a resolution demanding La Follette's resignation.

The New York Times for the second time in a week ran an article suggesting that La Follette was mentally imbalanced. The author retold the events of the Senator's 1912 debacle in Philadelphia and concluded, "The trouble with La Follette is that he has but one idea—to attack whatever is nearest, whatever is in good repute or ill-repute, provided it is near. He is a congenital attacker, a name-caller, a diatriber. He is a professional denouncer. . . . He is a sick man."[29]

---

[27]*NYT,* October 16, 1917, 3:5.

[28]*Ibid.,* October 17, 1917, 12:7.

[29]*NYT,* October 21, 1917, IX, 2:1 (article by Rupert Hughes).

90

The *Times* also accused La Follette of abusing his government postal privileges to undermine the sale of war bonds. The Senator responded that he never intended to hurt bond sales, but rather that his objective was to organize a campaign for higher taxation on war profits and surplus incomes. He asserted that while war profits in the United States were taxed at a rate of 31%, England taxed them at 80%. The press accounts of his activities were due to the fact that the it had "the interests of wealth especially in their keeping."

As October 1917, drew to a close, American troops appeared for the first time in the trenches on the Western front. At this juncture, when all he had warned against had come to pass, there arose an opportunity for La Follette's standing among Wisconsin voters to be tested. Paul Hustings, his Democratic colleague, was accidently killed while duck hunting. While the *Times* and other pro-war papers described Hustings as a foe of La Follette, Hustings had gone out of his way to avoid criticizing La Follette, although he had supported President Wilson at every turn. The *Times* proclaimed that "La Follette's candidate . . . should be opposed by an out and out American. . . . [T]he question [is] whether [Wisconsin] has chosen her country's side or the enemy's. . . ."[30]

Wisconsin was not the only place where the politicians would take advantage of their opponent's alleged lack of patriotism. In the electoral race for Mayor of New York, the incumbent, John P. Mitchel, accused his Democratic opponent, John F. Hylan, of "conspiring with the agents of Germany to create in this country a disloyal press." The Socialist candidate, Morris Hillquit, speaking to 12,000 supporters and several stenographers sent by the Department of Justice at Madison Square Garden, denounced both Mitchel and Hylan as pro-war.[31]

The intensity of the propaganda campaign against all those who opposed the war periodically escalated into violence. In Newport, Kentucky, a Congregationalist minister, Herbert S. Bigelow, was kidnapped, flogged and nearly lynched after giving a pacifist sermon at his

---

[30]*NYT,* October 23, 1917, 1:2; October 24, 1917, 14:1.

[31]*NYT,* November 1, 1917, 14:5.

91

church across the Ohio River in Cincinnati. Senator La Follette sent Bigelow a letter condemning the assault, and Lillian D. Wald, on behalf of the American Union Against Militarism, wired a telegram to President Wilson asking that he use his influence to stop such attacks.

Wald's telegram read:

> It is well-known that these acts have been committed in many instances not by obscure and irresponsible elements, but at the instigation of powerful interests and that the authorities have not been active in preventing them. One word from you will put an end to these outrages and to the vicious practice of many newspapers and organizations which openly encourage mob violence. For the third time we call upon you to speak this word, to charge Federal, State and City officials throughout the country that their first duty is to protect the people's rights.[32]

Although Secretary of War Newton P. Baker condemned the attack on Reverend Bigelow, no word in defense of the right to dissent was forthcoming from President Wilson. At least the President did not condone the attack as did *The New York Times*. The paper faulted Senator La Follette's note of sympathy to Bigelow because it "gave no consideration to the fact that the men who flogged Mr. Bigelow had been subjected to great provocation." The *Times* asked rhetorically where was Senator La Follette's empathy for the victims of German atrocities in Belgium, France, and on the high seas.[33]

In December 1917, eight months after the declaration of war against Germany, President Wilson got around to asking Congress for a similar declaration against Austria-Hungary. *The New York Times* reported that

---

[32]*NYT*, November 2, 1917, 24:5.

[33]*NYT*, November 13, 1917, 14:5. One of the most notorious examples of war hysteria was the lynching of a young German immigrant, Robert Prager, in Collinsville, Illinois, on April 5, 1918. No member of the mob who lynched Prager, simply because he had expressed pro-German sympathies and was generally disliked, was ever punished. Luebke, *Bonds of Loyalty*, Chapter One.

Bob La Follette kept his seat while other legislators cheered enthusiastically. The Senator voted against the declaration of war but explained afterwards that he would have voted for it if he had been able to amend the resolution. The declaration, he said, should state that the United States was not bound by any agreements with regard to Austrian-Hungarian territory in the event of an Allied victory.[34]

La Follette's failure to fall in line with the prevailing national sentiment began to have menacing repercussions in his home state by the end of 1917. At the end of December, he was expelled from the Madison Club, indicating wide-spread unpopularity even in his home city. In January 1918, the faculty of the University of Wisconsin adopted a resolution supporting President Wilson and condemning Senator La Follette. The passage of the faculty resolution was part of a break between La Follette and University President Charles Van Hise, a long-time supporter and close personal friend. Although La Follette parted company with a number of former political allies during the war, the end of his friendship with Van Hise was probably the most painful consequence of his stand from a personal point of view.[35]

With the barrage of criticism mounting and increasing demands for his resignation or expulsion from the Senate, La Follette was suddenly confronted with a grave personal crisis. At the end of January 1918,

---

[34]*NYT,* December 5, 1917, 2:4; December 8, 1917, 4:2.

[35]As noted later, there was a move in the Wisconsin legislature in 1923 to have the 1918 faculty resolution publicly destroyed as a gesture of apology. La Follette vigorously opposed this move by some of his supporters.

Many others had occasion to express their regrets over what they had written and said about La Follette during the war. The writer Irwin Cobb, who authored a hysterically anti-La Follette article in the *Saturday Evening Post*, had occasion to write George Middleton, the Senator's son-in-law in 1933:

> I have come to realize that the policies, which he so courageously advocated in the face of a then almost nationwide condemnation, were in the main right policies. We—all were blind, not he. We ran with the herd, he almost alone, risked his political future and for the moment sacrificed his political popularity, to stand fast by his honest opinions. Middleton, *These Things Are Mine,* p. 175.

Robert M. La Follette, Jr., became ill with streptococcic pneumonia. Senator La Follette would spend much of the next year caring for his son, and the illness may well have been beneficial politically. While the illness came very close to being fatal to Bob, Jr., the long absences of the senior La Follette from the Senate and public view, as well as some degree of sympathy, helped dampen some of the ardor of his detractors.

Just before the illness of his son, Senator La Follette had given his cautious approval to the speech that is the centerpiece of Woodrow Wilson's historical reputation. On January 8, 1918, Wilson enunciated his "Fourteen Points" on which the post-war order would be based. Although clear in demanding the evacuation of German troops from France, Belgium, and Russia and promising to France the return of the provinces of Alsace-Lorraine, which had been lost to Germany in 1871, the speech did not mention the payment of reparations to the Allies, which would in fact be the critical feature of the post-war peace.

One of the points called for the establishment of an independent Polish state with access to the sea. At Versailles, the decision to accomplish this end by giving Poland a corridor through German East Prussia, would provide one of the precipitating factors for World War II. However, an equally important factor was the direct contravention of point five which promised "a free, open-minded, and absolutely impartial adjustment of all colonial claims" with consideration of the interests of the colonial populations and the government claiming title. Nothing in the Fourteen Points was consistent with stripping Germany of all its colonies and dividing them up amongst the Allies.

At the end of the war, the Germans agreed to the armistice after assurances from Wilson that the final peace treaty between the Allies and Germany would be based on the Fourteen Points. La Follette in opposing Senate ratification of Wilson's Versailles Treaty would charge that German agreement to the armistice was induced by fraud. This view became almost universally held in post-war Germany.[36]

---

[36]This viewpoint, generally accepted in Germany, was vigorously contested by that country's former ambassador to Washington, Count von Bernstorff. The agreement to the armistice, said the Count, was dictated by the Supreme Army

Back in Wisconsin, a bitter fight was taking place for the U.S. Senate seat of the late Paul Hustings. La Follette's candidate for the Republican nomination was James Thompson, who promised to support vigorous prosecution of the war but supported a Congressional statement of U.S. war aims and much heavier taxes on war profits. The anti-La Follette Republicans nominated the Senator's former protege, Irvine Lenroot, to oppose Thompson. While the Democratic candidate, Joseph T. Davis, promised to vote for La Follette's expulsion from the Senate, both Lenroot and Thompson refused to respond to demands from the *Milwaukee Journal* that they announce how they intended to vote.

To embarrass La Follette and hurt Thompson's chances in the primary, both houses of the Wisconsin legislature passed resolutions denouncing the Senator just before the March 19, 1918, primary. The anti-La Follette resolution passed 22-7 in the Wisconsin Senate. A week later on March 6, the Wisconsin House passed the following resolution:

> The people of the State of Wisconsin always have stood and always will stand squarely behind the national Government in all things which are essential to bring the present war to a successful end, and we condemn Senator Robert La Follette and all others who have failed to see the righteousness of our nation's cause, who have failed to support our Government in matters vital to the winning of the war, and we denounce any attitude or utterance of theirs which has tended to incite sedition among the people of our country and to injure Wisconsin's fair name before the free people of the world.[37]

Command's declaration to the Kaiser that it could no longer hold back the advancing Allies on the Western front. The exchange of notes between Germany and the United States regarding the Fourteen Points was, according to Bernstorff, only a face-saving device. Bernstorff, *Memoirs,* p. 136. The Count's views on this and other matters necessitated his departure from Germany in 1933. He died in exile in Switzerland in 1939.

[37]*New York Times*, March 7, 1918, 1:3.

To the extent that the Republican primary can be considered a referendum on La Follette's popularity, it indicated that a narrow majority of his constituents disapproved of his views. Lenroot defeated Thompson 73,186 to 70,772.[38] However, upon winning the nomination, Lenroot immediately started courting La Follette's supporters for fear that their alienation might cost him the general election.

Vice President Thomas Marshall set the tone of the Democratic campaign in suggesting to Wisconsin voters that only a victory by the Democrat Davis would prove the state's loyalty to the rest of the nation. Democrats recalled that Lenroot had favored embargoing arms to the Allies in 1915. While the Republican candidate had to distance himself somewhat from La Follette, he feared that if he did so excessively, enough of those Republicans who voted for Thompson might vote for the third candidate in the race, Socialist Victor Berger, and throw the election to Davis.[39] On April 3, 1918, Lenroot emerged from the special election victorious. The early balloting gave him 142,000 votes to 132,000 for Davis. The Socialist Berger polled 96,000 votes.[40]

At the end of May 1918, the Pomerene Committee entertained two hours of argument from Senator La Follette's counsel, Gilbert Roe. Roe asked that the charges against his client be dropped, alleging that they were based largely on the incorrect report of the Senator's St. Paul speech by the Associated Press. He argued that the Senator had made no erroneous statements because the *Lusitania* had carried arms in her hold.

Roe succeeded in shifting the focus from Senator La Follette to the Associated Press. The news agency telegraphed Senator Pomerene on May 23, conceding that its report of the St. Paul address had been erroneous.

---

[38]Fola La Follette, *Robert M. La Follette*, Vol II., p. 869.

[39]*NYT*, March 27, 1918, 11:3.; March 31, 1918, I 8:1.; April 1, 1918, 6:4.

[40]*NYT*, April 4, 1918, 5:3. Lenroot, with a little more luck, could have ended his political career as President of the United States. In 1920, he was a leading contender for the Republican Vice-Presidential nomination. The party leadership chose Massachusetts Governor Calvin Coolidge instead, who became Chief Executive upon the death of President Harding in 1923.

Hard core La Follette-haters, such as the editors of *The New York Times* argued that the AP error was inconsequential since the tenor of La Follette's speech was that the grievances that America had against Germany were trivial. Nevertheless, Roe succeeded in convincing many that the treason charges were based on faulty information.[41]

News that Robert La Follette, Jr., was critically ill at the end of July further dampened any effort to expedite Senate consideration of the expulsion resolution. The Senator's other son, Philip, entered an army officer training program at Ft. Sheridan, Illinois. The Senator, fearing retaliation because of his notoriety, had advised the boy to join the marines, where he believed that his son would be protected from harassment by Navy Secretary Josephus Daniels.[42]

The exchange of letters between the Senator and his younger son expresses the ambivalence of both regarding a citizen's obligation to serve in a war of which he disapproves. Philip told his father that he could not register as a conscientious objector because his objection to the war had no religious basis. He also ruled out returning to the family farm on the grounds that all his father's enemies would charge him with avoiding the draft. He ultimately took an Army commission but was discharged a few months later when the war ended.[43]

---

[41]*NYT,* May 25, 1918, 12:1.

[42]Senator La Follette wrote Philip regarding "very dear messages" from Daniels, expressing confidence in him and emphatically disapproving of the attacks made against the Wisconsin Senator. La Follette Family Papers, Library of Congress, Letter of May 26, 1918, Container A 22. *Also see* Young, ed., *Adventures in Politics, The Memoirs of Philip La Follette*, pp. 56-70.

[43]Philip La Follette to his father, May 19, 1918, La Follette Family Papers, Library of Congress, Container A22. In World War II, Philip La Follette volunteered for military service and served as a Colonel on the staff of General Douglas MacArthur. Always more independent of his father than his older brother, Bob, Jr., the above cited letter shows an early inclination to form views that did not necessarily follow from his father's. He wrote:
During the first year it seemed possible that Germany would accept a fair peace if offered her. [However] her treatment of Russia shook that belief.

97

By September 1918, the infusion of hundreds of thousands of fresh American troops was making itself felt on the Western front. The German offensive of the spring had come close to breaking the Allied lines but had fallen short of achieving victory. In the latter stages of the German thrust, the Americans played a significant role in shoring up the French and British defenses. Then the Allies went on the offensive. As they pushed forward, American troops captured St. Mihiel and were in the vicinity of Metz in Alsace-Lorraine.

The Central Powers, which just a few months before had believed themselves on the verge of victory, lost their confidence. Austria-Hungary sent a peace proposal to President Wilson, which he firmly rejected. With General Pershing calling for several million more American troops for an offensive planned for the spring of 1919, many in Berlin and Vienna were beginning to see that American intervention had made their ultimate defeat an inevitability.

With victory in sight and the 1918 congressional elections approaching, the Senate Committee on Privileges and Elections voted on September 26, 1918, to delay consideration of the resolution to expel La Follette until after the elections. Only Chairman Pomerene voted against delay.[44]

In late October, President Wilson appealed to the nation to elect a Democratic Congress on the grounds that this was necessary for achieving victory. The strategy backfired as the Republicans depicted the President

---

But regardless of that fact, it is evident that we must not permit Germany to win on the Western front, and that we must obtain an honorable peace.

[44]*NYT,* September 27, 1918, 11:5. The same day the Senate was debating women's suffrage. The *Times* reported that suffragettes were waiting for the return to the Senate of La Follette and Hiram Johnson of California before bringing the matter to a vote. John Sharp Williams of Mississippi wanted the amendment limited to white women. Senator Vardaman supported his colleague but said he would vote for women's suffrage, even if it applied to all women. Of course, in much of the South, black men had already been disenfranchised so that the political effect of the black women's vote was a moot point. The supposedly progressive Atlee Pomerene of Ohio was an opponent of women's suffrage.

as having been slow to recognize the peril of German victory and not sufficiently anti-German to be trusted in concluding peace with Berlin. The Republicans scored heavy gains and captured control of both the Senate and the House. While their margin in the House was comfortable, they held the Senate by the narrow margin of 49 to 47. It therefore became critical to the Republican leadership that La Follette and his close allies, like Gronna and Norris, continued to count themselves as a Republicans so that the party could organize the Senate and take control of the committee chairmanships.

All of a sudden, some very reactionary Republicans, particularly Henry Cabot Lodge of Massachusetts, began to see some redeeming qualities in Robert M. La Follette. If the Wisconsin Senator and his small band of supporters stayed on the Republican side of the Senate, the chairmanship of the Foreign Relations Committee would pass from Democrat Gilbert Hitchcock to Lodge. If just La Follette and Gronna defected from the Republican ranks, the Democrats might retain control of the Committee. If La Follette were expelled from the Senate and a Democrat were to win the special election to replace him, Lodge's ambitions would also not be well served.

Of the six Senators who voted against American entry into the war, only Vardaman and George Norris had to run for re-election in 1918. Vardaman paid for his opposition to the war by being defeated by Congressman Pat Harrison, a supporter of the war, in the Democratic primary. Norris was re-elected in Nebraska, which raises the question of whether La Follette could have survived an electoral challenge in 1918 or 1920. Surprisingly, Norris' principal opponent in the Republican primary, Congressman Charles H. Sloan, had been one of the 50 representatives to vote against the war.

Norris received 23,000 votes to Sloan's 17,000, with other candidates receiving as many votes as Norris. It appears that had Norris' opponents unified behind a suitable opponent, he would have lost. In the general election, the Senator defeated his Democratic opponent 120,000 to 99,960[45]

[45]Nueberger, Richard and Kahn, Stephen B., *Integrity, The Life of George W. Norris,* p. 132.

A few days after the election, on November 11, 1918, the Germans agreed to the armistice, and the guns fell silent in Europe. Two weeks later the Senate Committee on Privileges and Elections voted 9 to 2 to abandon its investigation of La Follette's St. Paul address. Among the majority were Vardaman, the sympathetic Sherman from Illinois, Reed, the lukewarm war supporter from Missouri, and even Republican Senator Kellogg, who had introduced the expulsion petition in the Senate. While Kellogg may have had other reasons for voting to drop the investigation, the arithmetic of the Republican control over the new Senate could not have escaped him.

The two voting to continue the investigation were Committee Chairman Pomerene and Democrat Thomas Walsh of Montana, who in a few years would become one of La Follette's closest political allies during the investigation of the Teapot Dome Scandal. Bob, Jr., wrote the Senator, "I suppose old Pomerene and Walsh just felt that they had to hang together in a last effort to save their faces, if possible."[46]

Pomerene issued a minority report to the Committee's report. In a very confusing manner, he postulated that once the United States has declared war a Senator has even a greater duty than the average citizen to avoid criticism of government policy or advocate any change to that policy. He intimated that La Follette may have deserved expulsion solely for failing to subscribe to the views of the majority as to the origins of American intervention in the European war.

Indeed, in some portions of his report, the Ohio Senator made accusations that, if anything, proved La Follette's point. For instance, he charged that in the St. Paul speech "[La Follette] wholly ignores the real causes which led to the war. . . . He ignores the fact that compliance with the German Imperial Government's order . . . that after February 1, 1917,

---

[46]Robert M. La Follette, Jr., to his father, November 24, 1918, La Follette Family Papers, Container A 22, Library of Congress.

all vessels which appeared in the war zone would be sunk, would . . . deny to 110,000,000 people a foreign commerce aggregating $6,000,000,000 annually."[47]

Pomerene then asked, "[w]hat excuse has the Senator for these statements? I have heard none." To the contrary, Pomerene had heard La Follette argue many times that it was wrong to go to war with Germany for denying America its right to trade with the Allies, when we had never taken any effective action against Britain for denying us our rights to trade with Germany. Further, for Pomerene to even mention the financial impact of complying with the Kaiser's blockade was to concede La Follette's premise that the real reason for going to war was America's economic stake in Allied victory, rather than any matter of principle.

Mrs. La Follette's feelings towards the Ohio Senator were contained in a letter to her children in which she stated, "Pomerene has been as low and mean and cowardly as he could be. How he could have the gall to make such a report in view of the record, I cannot understand."[48]

The euphoria of the Allied triumph was lost on the Wisconsin Senator. Within a few days of the armistice, he was predicting to his family that President Wilson would quickly abandon the Fourteen Points and that victory would merely sow the seeds of a future war. He concluded "all we are going to have left is peace, a big war debt, and Wilson's speeches.[49]

La Follette's grim assessment as to the long-term effect of the Allied victory turned out to be largely correct. However, nobody could have anticipated the turn of events that made it so. The German politicans who thought that they were saving their nation from complete ruin by making

---

[47]Calendar No. 560, 65th Cong., 3d Sess., Rpt. 614, Part 2, Senate "Views of a Minority."

[48]Letter Belle Case La Follette to family December 16, 1918, La Follette Family Papers, Container A 22, Library of Congress.

[49]*Robert M. La Follette*, Vol. II, pp. 907-8.

peace in 1918 were rewarded with vilification by their countrymen and, in some cases, assassination. They became commonly referred to as "the November criminals."

Generals Ludendorff and Hindenberg conveniently forgot their many miscalculations during the war and that they had advised the Kaiser that the war was lost in the fall of 1918. They succeeded in propagating possibly the greatest lie in all of history—that the war had been lost by domestic traitors and that without this treachery the war would have been won.

The majority of the German people were sick of the war in 1918 and were pleased with the armistice. Within fifteen years, however, they came to accept as fact that the war had been lost because their nation had been betrayed and that all their Jewish countrymen were parties to this betrayal. Acceptance of the lie required blinders to the truth. The fact is that if Germany had not lost the war in 1918, it would most certainly have lost it in 1919.

The Allied blockade made continuation of the war increasingly difficult. The Germans could not have contained the millions of fresh American soldiers that General Pershing planned to throw against them in the spring of 1919. Indeed, the Kaiser's army was barely holding its own against the Allied troops already at the front in the fall of 1918.

The Germans' capacity for self-deception would not have produced World War II, however, had it not been for the great economic depression of the 1930s. The political fortunes of Adolf Hitler prove that without economic chaos, the world might have weathered the upheaval produced by World War I and the Versailles Peace Conference. Hitler, who survived four years on the Western front as a corporal in a Bavarian regiment, was a serious threat to the German national government by 1923. With a little more luck, his Beer Hall Putsch in November of that year may well have replicated Mussolini's feat of capturing control of Italy.

However, by 1928, Hitler was a political has-been. In the national elections, his Nazis gathered only 2% of the vote. The Depression, however, re-opened the old wounds of 1918-1919, and, in 1932, the Nazis received 37% of the vote and were Germany's largest political party. After failure of one government after another, President Hindenburg entrusted his nation to Hitler, a man whose political faith rested on two principles; a desire to eliminate the Jews from German life, and a determination to destroy the vestiges of the 1918 armistice and the Versailles conference.

The New York Tribune, September 25, 1917, "The Enemy Aboard"

CHAPTER 6
The Post-War World

On January 7, 1919, La Follette made his first Senate speech on international affairs in over a year. He objected to the continued presence of American troops in Russia. No declaration of war, La Follette claimed, justified their presence there. Senator Claude Swanson replied that American troops were needed to guard U.S. munitions in Russia until a final peace treaty was signed with Germany. Hitchcock of Nebraska took issue with La Follette as to whether the Bolshevik government of Russia was pro-German, ignoring the harsh peace terms forced upon the Communists by the Kaiser's government at Brest-Litovsk in March 1918. He also overlooked the fact that the government with which we had been at war had ceased to exist two months earlier when the Kaiser abdicated his throne and fled to Holland.[1]

On January 16, 1919, Senator Dillingham, a Republican from Vermont, offered a resolution stating that La Follette's St. Paul speech did not justify any action by the Senate. His resolution passed by a vote of 50 to 21. Thirty-three Republicans and 17 Democrats voted to end La Follette's ordeal. The 21 opposed included only one Republican, Smith of Michigan. Prominent among the Democrats opposed were Pomerene, Walsh, and John Sharp Williams of Mississippi. Included in the majority were Lodge, Kellogg, La Follette's new rival in his home state, Irvine Lenroot, and the conservative Senator Wadsworth from New York.

However, before the Dillingham resolution was brought to a vote, La Follette had to endure one of the bitterest personal attacks ever made by one Senator upon another—from John Sharp Williams. While La Follette sat passively with his hands on his knees, Williams angrily screamed at him, "[I]t is an everlasting lie that the United States went to war to protect any Morgan interests or any capitalistic interests of any sort . . . . It is an

---

[1]*New York Times,* January 18, 1919, 3:3; January 10, 1919, 4:1.

105

everlasting lie that the *Lusitania* was armed or had any dangerous explosives aboard. . . ."[2]

The New York Times expressed its sympathy for Williams the next day and the hope that La Follette's "misconception of public opinion in his opposition to the war may teach him to be more careful in the future." To the contrary, the expulsion attempt made Bob La Follette more radical and more aggressive than ever.

A week later, the Senator was one of 18 who voted against a $100 million aid bill for European famine relief. La Follette was angry that the measure allotted no help to the Germans and charged that the measure was simply an attempt by American meat packers to enrich themselves at the public trough.[3] In early March, he spoke for four hours as part of a Republican filibuster against Wilson's Victory Bond Authorization Bill. Tempers flared to the point that La Follette and Democrat Joseph Robinson almost came to blows.[4]

The attention of the American people during the first months after the war was monopolized by their President. Less than a month after the war ended, Wilson left for Paris, where he was received as the savior of mankind. In a political blunder of the first order, he declined to include any prominent Republicans in the delegation he took with him to the Versailles Peace Conference.[5] At Versailles, he found that the Allies, particularly the French, who paid incomparably more for victory than the Americans, were in no mood to be lenient with Germany—Kaiser or no Kaiser.

---

[2]*NYT,* January 17, 1919, 11:3.

[3]*NYT,* January 25, 1919, 6:2.

[4]*NYT,* March 2, 1919, 1:8.

[5]The American delegation to the peace conference included one Republican, Henry White, a man with no particular influence in his party. The other delegates were Wilson, General Tasker Bliss, Secretary of State Robert Lansing, and the President's confidant without portfolio, "Colonel" Edward M. House.

All the heavy-handed sanctions imposed upon the Germans at Versailles, territorial adjustments and monetary reparations, had ample precedent in Germany's treatment of France in 1870. However, they neither boded well for the survival of democracy in Germany, nor made Woodrow Wilson appear particularly principled after all his high-minded pronouncements during the war about having no quarrel with the German people. Wilson's hopes for a new world order with American leadership of the League of Nations was thwarted by Senatorial Republicans for primarily domestic political reasons. However, the feeling of Robert La Follette and others that the President had not dealt in good faith with the Germans was also a significant factor in his defeat.

Upon the President's return from France in the summer of 1919, La Follette lambasted him with an editorial in his magazine entitled "Wilson's Broken Pledges." He wrote his sons that "I sometimes think the man [Wilson] has no sense of things that penetrate below the surface. With him the rhetoric of a thing is the thing itself. . . ."[6]

On September 3, 1919, the President began a cross-country tour to rally popular opinion to his side in the battle with the Senate Republicans over the Treaty of Versailles and the League of Nations. Three weeks later he suffered a stroke, which ended his tour and left him incapacitated for most of the remaining year and a half of his presidency.

On November 18, 1919, a day on which the newspapers heralded the fact that the President was well enough to appear on the White House lawn in a wheelchair, his former admirer, Robert La Follette, had to be cut off after a hour-long speech demanding that the President's Fourteen Points be considered binding with regard to the Versailles treaty. He proposed six reservations to the treaty:

1. An explicit prohibition of any U.S. aid in suppressing native rebellions in India, Ireland, Korea, Egypt, or other colonial nations;

2. A provision for the withdrawal of the United States from the League of Nations within one year if the member states failed to abolish conscription;

---

[6] *Robert M. La Follette*, Vol. II, p. 967.

3. Another provision requiring the United States to withdraw from the League unless all member states required a national referendum as a precondition for going to war;

4. A requirement for all nations to reduce armaments, particularly (with England obviously in mind) their navies;

5. Withdrawal of the United States from the League if any member attempted to acquire the territory of a non-member (obviously aimed at France's desire for territory held by Germany prior to 1914); and

6. Withdrawal of the United States from the League if any member state appropriated the resources of a nation over which it exercised a mandate or protectorate.[7]

On the next day came the showdown between Woodrow Wilson and Henry Cabot Lodge. The Senate first voted on ratification of the Treaty of Versailles with reservations proposed by Lodge. The Massachusetts Senator's version of the treaty would have preserved the United States' right to interpret and apply the Monroe Doctrine unilaterally and to decide what issues were domestic concerns outside the purview of the League of Nations. Lodge's desire to restrict immigration and impose protective tariffs for American manufacturers were among his principal concerns.

However, the major issue was Lodge's proposed reservation to Article X of the League of Nations Covenant. As stated in the treaty concluded at Versailles, the article provided that

> [T]he members of the League undertake to respect and preserve as against external aggression the territorial integrity and existing political independence of all Members of the League. In case of any such aggression or in any case of any threat or danger of such aggression the [League] Council shall advise upon the means by which this obligation shall be fulfilled.

---

[7]*NYT,* November 19, 1919, 1:7.

The Lodge reservation proclaimed that the United States assumed no obligation under Article X unless Congress by act or joint resolution agreed to assume such obligations.

Wilson instructed the Senate Democrats to accept the treaty he had brought back from Paris, or nothing. The treaty with the Lodge reservations was defeated by a vote of 55 to 39, and upon a motion to reconsider 50 to 41. Then the treaty brought back by Wilson from Versailles came before the Senate. It was voted down 53 to 38. The Progressive Republicans, La Follette, Norris, Gronna, Borah, and Hiram Johnson, voted against the Treaty in any form. Even a few Democrats voted against the Wilson treaty, most notably Oklahoma's Thomas Gore and Missouri's James Reed, two very lukewarm supporters of Wilson's war policies. While Ohio Senator Warren G. Harding blamed the failure of treaty ratification on Wilson's unwillingness to compromise with the Republicans, it is possible that Lodge would have insisted on just enough concessions to guarantee that Wilson would never agree with him.[8]

The defeat of Wilson's cherished League of Nations was a critical part of the jockeying for position for the upcoming presidential election in 1920. Unexpectedly, the most probable Republican candidate, 60-year-old Theodore Roosevelt, the pathological Wilson-hater, died after a brief illness in January 1919. In December of that year, the Republican state conventions endorsed Roosevelt's alter ego, General Leonard Wood, as

---

[8]One who took issue with the portrayal of Lodge as an obstructionist was his grandson. Henry Cabot Lodge, Jr., was a Senator from Massachusetts until his defeat by John F. Kennedy in 1952, then UN ambassador, and Richard Nixon's running mate in 1960. Professor John A. Garrity invited Ambassador Lodge to comment on his biography of Lodge, Sr., and included these comments as footnotes to his book. Ambassador Lodge argued with some force that his grandfather's reservations to the League of Nations Covenant were essential to making it consistent with the United States Constitution and contended that the UN charter was much more consistent with his grandfather's version of the Covenant than with Wilson's.

109

their preferred presidential candidate. Democratic party gatherings endorsed the incapacitated Wilson for a third term.[9]

That La Follette's popularity in Wisconsin was recovering from the decline it suffered during the war was demonstrated by the victory of his slate of delegates in the April 1920 primary contest for delegates to the Republican national convention. The Senator himself was to play no role in the convention itself, as he was forced to have his gall bladder removed only a few days before it began. A La Follette lieutenant, Edwin Grose, was greeted with hisses and boos when he presented the Senator's views to the convention. La Follette's demands for government ownership of the railroads and stockyards drew a particularly hostile response. Grose also presented a ringing denunciation of the Versailles Treaty as a betrayal of the hopes of mankind and a request for support of Irish independence.[10]

On the first ballot, General Wood led all candidates with 287½ votes; Governor Frank Lowden of Illinois was second with 211½, the Progressive Hiram Johnson of California was third with 133½, and Senator Warren G. Harding of Ohio, whose main virtue was his lack of enemies, was fourth with 65½. La Follette received 24 of Wisconsin's 26 votes, but no others.

With the leading candidates adamantly opposed to the nomination of any of their major rivals, the party settled on Harding as its nominee on the 10th ballot and Governor Calvin Coolidge of Massachusetts as its Vice-Presidential nominee. Almost immediately, a group of disgruntled progressives, calling themselves the Committee of 48 proposed a possible third-party candidacy by La Follette.[11]

In July, the Democrats after being deadlocked between President Wilson's son-in-law, Treasury Secretary William G. McAdoo, and Ohio Governor James A. Cox, selected Cox. As the Vice-Presidential nominee, the convention selected a McAdoo supporter, the young Assistant Secretary of the Navy, Franklin Delano Roosevelt. Talk of a third party increased

---

[9]*NYT,* December 3, 1919, 1:3.

[10]*NYT,* June 7, 1920, 5:3; June 11, 1920, 2:8.

[11]*NYT,* June 12, 1920, 1:8; June 13, 1920, 1:8; June 14, 1920, 1:5.

after the Democratic convention with La Follette as the first choice of most of the disgruntled progressives.

On July 14, 1920, La Follette announced that he would accept the nomination of a third party if its platform was acceptable. While it's doubtful that anyone expected that such a candidacy would be successful, both major parties were unacceptable to progressives. With Harding, the Republican party had clearly been captured by its most conservative element, completely sympathetic with big business. The major transgression of the Democratic ticket was its determination to vindicate the foreign policy of Woodrow Wilson and to gain American entry into the League of Nations on his terms.

A July convention of progressives and socialists adopted a platform that was too far to the left for La Follette, who declined the nomination. The more leftist element of the convention nominated Parley Christensen as the Farmer-Labor candidate for President. Other efforts at forming a less radical progressive ticket with La Follette failed, but the seeds of his 1924 candidacy had been sown.

In the early fall of 1920, Senator La Follette was far more concerned with the battle for control of the Republican party in Wisconsin than the national election, since he had little enthusiasm for either Presidential candidate. His most acute interest was in defeating the incumbent Senator Irvine Lenroot in the Republican primary. In this regard, La Follette was unsuccessful as Lenroot won the Republican nomination by a margin of 35,000 over La Follette's candidate, James Thompson. The 1920 primary was not, however, a complete defeat for La Follette. His candidate for Governor, John J. Blaine, was victorious, and La Follette succeeded in defeating Congressman John J. Esch, the principal opponent of public ownership or control of the railroads in the House of Representatives.

Late in the campaign, La Follette gave a half-hearted endorsement to Harding's Presidential bid. He attacked the Wilson administration as a failure and charged that Wilson and Cox's League of Nations would barter away American independence. The Senator predicted a Republican victory in November but warned that the reactionary element in the party would seek to control Harding, as he felt they had controlled Taft.

111

Nevertheless, La Follette's conciliatory mood towards the Republican party had its limits. As to Senator Lenroot, La Follette declared, "I cannot support a man who voted for the Espionage law, by which hundreds of loyal citizens were persecuted—a man who won his nomination by deceit and duplicity."[12]

In November, the nation overwhelmingly rejected Woodrow Wilson. Governor Cox, forced to run his campaign as a referendum on Wilson's League of Nations, was soundly defeated by Warren G. Harding, who promised the nation a "return to normalcy." That Harding was no progressive was hardly a surprise to La Follette, and almost immediately he locked horns with the new President over his nomination of ex-Congressman Esch to the Interstate Commerce Commission.

The New York Times counseled Senate Republicans to ignore La Follette's objections to Esch and to regard Senator Lenroot as the true head of the Republican party in Wisconsin. La Follette, said the *Times,* was an "assistant Democrat."[13] Few Senators of either party paid attention to La Follette's objection to Esch, whom he characterized as a tool of the railroads, and confirmed the nomination by a vote of 52–3.

In May 1921, the German government finally caved in to Allied demands and agreed to sign the Versailles treaty. La Follette immediately introduced a resolution in the Senate denouncing the treaty as "a crime born of blind revenge and insatiable greed" and said that it was a betrayal of the promises made by the United States government. In response to President Harding's acceptance of an invitation to appoint American representatives to the Allied Supreme Council, the Council of Ambassadors, and the Reparations Commission, La Follette's resolution declared that American participation would be contrary to this country's ideals and principles. These councils, he warned, were simply devices by

---

[12]*NYT,* October 22, 1920, 3:4.

[13]*NYT,* March 21, 1921, 12:1.

which America would give its sanction to Allied imperialism in Europe, Asia, and Africa.[14]

The New York Times' comment on La Follette's resolution indicates that it regarded the Wisconsin Senator an ineffective windbag. The *Times* observed that isolationists such as Borah of Idaho and Hiram Johnson of California probably shared La Follette's views but were precluded from stating them because they had been publicly espoused by La Follette:

> Imagine their rage at being frustrated by the infuriating La Follette with his resolution. He says what they would have said, but by saying it first he makes it impossible for them to say anything in the same vein. They cannot follow where he leads, for they hate him as though he were League of Nations. . . .[15]

One has to wonder why the *Times* spewed forth so much venom in La Follette's direction—if it did not think he had any influence and was completely harmless.

In addition to making life difficult for President Harding and his Secretary of State, Charles Evans Hughes, La Follette continued to press for progressive taxation and campaigned against the repeal of the wartime excess profits tax. The Senator also led the fight against huge increases in the appropriations for the U.S. Navy. La Follette charged that the major steel companies were behind the agitation for increased naval spending, and that their motivation was profit, rather than patriotism. Even La Follette's old nemesis, Senator Pomerene, expressed opposition to the build-up, suggesting it could only be justified on the absurd notion that the U.S. might some day go to war with Great Britain, the only nation with a navy stronger than America's.

La Follette's lack of party loyalty was evidenced in July 1921, when he was one of only four senators who voted against the confirmation of

---

[14]*NYT,* May 11, 1921, 19:1.

[15]*NYT,* May 12, 1921, 16:2.

former President William Howard Taft to be Chief Justice of the United States Supreme Court. Curiously, three of the four Senators voting against the nomination were Republicans, La Follette, Borah, and Hiram Johnson. The populist Democratic demagogue from Georgia, Tom Watson, was the fourth.[16]

His persecution during the war seemed to make Senator La Follette increasingly hostile to Great Britain. An indication as to the depth of his hostility is the following telegram he sent to a gathering of supporters of the Irish Republic meeting at Madison Square Garden in New York City:

> British diplomacy demands that the United States shall be an associate in Great Britain's plan to rule the world or else to be removed from her path as a rival. Patriotic men and women in the United States must be on guard against the avowed purpose to make the United States a party in British plans to control and exploit the rest of the world. I hope this assemblage will announce to the respective rulers of Great Britain and the United States that any scheme of conquest and dominion over other countries is abhorrent alike to the people of the United States and of Ireland and that to the last man they will resist any attempt to establish an imperialistic coalition between the United States and Great Britain.[17]

In addition to being wary of America's cozy relationship with England in Europe, La Follette also saw Harding and Hughes as turning the United States into a partner in European imperialism in the Far East. In December 1921, the U.S. signed a treaty with England, France, and Japan, pledging mutual respect of each's possessions in the Pacific. The terms of the treaty provided that the signatories were to consult with each other if the rights of any one of them was threatened by the aggressive action of any other power. La Follette immediately attacked the treaty as making

---

[16]*NYT,* July 1, 1921, 1:6.

[17]*NYT,* October 16, 1921, 19:2.

the U.S. an ally in every possible conflict in the Pacific involving the interests of any of the other signatories and called for its repudiation by the Senate.[18]

In Milwaukee in February 1922, La Follette charged that the four-power treaty had only one objective—"to make the world safe for imperialism." The American people, he stated, must decide whether to "follow the path along which Woodrow Wilson and Warren G. Harding have attempted to lead them, of becoming a great Western empire, a party to all the world's intrigues, hated by all peoples, respected by none." The agreement reached by the Harding administration, he concluded, was "nothing more or less than a binding alliance with the three great imperialistic nations of the present time, which pledges the United States to place all her resources of men and money at their disposal whenever they are attacked."[19]

Unlike his predecessor, President Harding had the foresight to include both Republican and Democratic leaders in the Senate in the team negotiating with the foreign powers. Thus, when the treaty came before the Senate for ratification, the President had significant Democratic support—since he was not trying to claim all the credit for the treaty for his party.

The Democrat Pomerene was the principal speaker for the treaty in the Senate debate. He took particular pains to defuse the charges of opponents that Japan was the principal beneficiary of the treaty. La Follette in response argued that the purpose of the treaty was to secure for the Japanese the "cordial co-operation" of the United States in its exploitation of China, Korea, and Siberia. He predicted that someday China, Germany, and Russia would retaliate against those who united to oppress and exploit them when they were weak.[20]

---

[18]*NYT*, December 14, 1921, 1:2, 2:4.

[19]*NYT*, February 20, 1922, 11:2; February 21, 1922, 16:1.

[20]*NYT*, March 23, 1922, 1:2.

On March 24, 1922, the treaty was ratified by a vote of 67-22, with a reservation that the United States understood that the treaty imposed no commitment to armed force, no alliance, and no obligation to join in any military defense of the other nations' possessions. Twelve Democrats, including Pomerene, John Sharp Williams, and Oscar Underwood (the latter having been part of the administrations's negotiating team), joined 55 Republicans in voting for the treaty. Twenty-three Democrats and four Republicans, including La Follette, Borah, and Hiram Johnson (who was virulently anti-Japanese) voted against ratification.[21]

While La Follette was clearly an ineffectual voice in the wilderness with regard to changing the direction of either American domestic or foreign policy, he introduced a resolution in the Senate in late April 1922, that initiated the uncovering of one of the greatest political scandals in American history. Interior Secretary Albert Fall had just announced that he leased government-owned oil fields in Wyoming and California, previously held in reserve for use by the navy, to oilmen Edward Doheny and Harry Sinclair.

Opponents of the leases had searched in vain for a political figure to make the leases an issue until they approached La Follette. In addition to his long-standing mistrust of big business and the Harding administration, La Follette had a particular dislike of Secretary Fall. The Interior Secretary was a former U.S. Senator from New Mexico, who La Follette thought had used his Senate seat exclusively for the advancement of his financial interests and those of his friends.

La Follette introduced a resolution calling for a Senate inquiry into all the facts surrounding the leases, which passed unanimously. He called Fall's Interior Department a "sluiceway for 90% of the corruption in this country," and asked how the President, in view of Fall's record, could have transferred control of the government oil fields from the Navy Department to Interior.

The major argument in favor of the leases was the assertion that the government fields were being drained by exploitation of adjacent privately owned fields, and thus it was in the government's best interests to allow

---

[21]*NYT*, March 25, 1922, 1:2-2:2.

private exploitation of its fields, while the oil was still beneath them. Until La Follette's entrance into the fray, the Senate had been willing to accept the assertions made by Fall's department on the drainage issue uncritically. La Follette, however, had spent considerable time with technical experts who knew that the government oilfields did not have to be immediately exploited to be saved and his championing of their cause persuaded the Senate to look into the matter.[22]

Pursuant to the La Follette resolution, an investigation into the leases was made by a Senate Committee headed by Democrat Thomas Walsh of Montana. The committee found strong indications that Interior Secretary Fall had been bribed by Doheny and Sinclair to lease the government oilfields to their companies. Calvin Coolidge, who had become President upon Harding's sudden death in 1923, then appointed two special prosecutors to seek cancellation of the leases and to initiate criminal proceedings.

Over La Follette's objections, one of the special prosecutors was former Senator Atlee Pomerene. The other special prosecutor was the future Supreme Court Justice Owen Roberts. The government was ultimately successful in having the leases cancelled. While Doheny and Sinclair were never incarcerated for their role in this affair, former Interior Secretary Fall became the first person in American history to go to jail for crimes committed while a Cabinet member. The scandal also is primarily responsible for the extremely poor historical reputation of the Harding Administration.

By mid-1922, both La Follette's friends and enemies began preparing for the Senator's re-election campaign. Obviously, one question was whether his stand against the war had damaged his standing with Wisconsin voters. Another issue was the increasingly leftward movement of the Senator on domestic issues. Opponents within the Republican party announced in June 1922 that they would fight La Follette's renomination on the issue of Communism. These detractors charged that by making

[22]*NYT,* April 22, 1922, 15:1; April 29, 1922, 1:2. In his attack on the leases, La Follette charged that naval officers opposed to the exploitation of the navy oil reserves had been reassigned to silence them.

common cause with Victor Berger and the Wisconsin Socialists, La Follette was paving the way for a Communist state.[23]

In seeking re-election, Senator La Follette made no effort to become less controversial; in fact, he became more radical. In 1922, he launched an all-out attack on the United States Supreme Court because of a number of decisions by the Taft Court that angered the Progressives. The Court had ruled in favor of United States Steel Corporation, holding that its size did not violate the anti-trust laws. La Follette called the decision the epitaph of the Sherman Act.

Shortly thereafter, the court ruled a new federal child labor law unconstitutional and in another case held that labor unions were subject to the anti-trust laws and were liable for damages caused by strikes. With regard to union liability for damages, Chief Justice Taft dismissed a suit by Coronado Coal Company against the United Mine Workers for lack of federal jurisdiction. However, he indicated that if the court had jurisdiction he would have affirmed a lower court judgment against the miners.

La Follette, never an admirer of the ex-President, was livid. He issued a statement proclaiming that the "court went out of its way to change the law as it has existed in this country since the beginning of the Government, that unincorporated associations, such as are involved here, could not be sued as an entity."[24] A week later, La Follette appeared as the principal speaker during a "child labor protest session" at the convention of the American Federation of Labor in Cincinnati. It is worth noting that Samuel Gompers, head of the AF of L, had been an enthusiastic supporter of President Wilson's war policy and a outspoken foe of all opponents of the war. By 1922, however, Gompers had no hesitation in embracing Senator La Follette.

Before the AF of L convention, the Wisconsin Senator called for a constitutional amendment to prohibit any federal judge other than a Supreme Court Justice from passing on the constitutionality of

---

[23]*NYT,* June 22, 1922, 3:6.

[24]*NYT,* June 8, 1922, 32:1.

congressional legislation. Even more importantly, he called for a provision that would allow Congress to nullify any decision of the Supreme Court regarding the constitutionality of legislation—simply by repassing the law.

La Follette correctly noted that nothing in the federal Constitution specifically gave the Court the authority to pass upon the constitutionality of federal legislation. However, such implicit power, first asserted by Chief Justice John Marshall over one hundred years earlier, had never been seriously challenged.[25]

The Senator's remarks quickly drew fire from his detractors and the business community. Nicholas Murray Butler, President of Columbia University, charged before the New Jersey Bar Association that La Follette was waging war on the American system of government.[26] La Follette responded with an *ad hominem* attack of his own, stating that President Butler "happens to be at the head of Columbia University, sustained by private contributions, a bootlicker of men of fortune in order that he may continue to obtain endowments to that institution to serve privilege."[27]

La Follette opened his re-election campaign with a speech in Milwaukee on July 6. He told his audience that he'd been advised to avoid mentioning the war in his campaign but defiantly proclaimed that he was proud of his stand and wouldn't change it with anyone.[28] In ensuing days, he emphasized his opposition to the Republican tariff bill—which was unpopular with farmers and organized labor.[29] His campaign against the tariff demonstrated how far La Follette had come from his days as a Republican party loyalist under the tutelage of William McKinley. When he was in Congress between 1884 and 1890, support for protective tariffs was what separated a Republican from a Democrat.

---

[25]*NYT,* June 15, 1922, 1:2.

[26]*NYT,* June 17, 1922, 12:8.

[27]*NYT,* June 22, 1922, 9:7.

[28]*Robert M. La Follette,* Vol II, p. 1059.

[29]*NYT,* July 8, 1922, 1:2; July 9, 1922, 4:1.

Anti-La Follette Republicans selected Dr. William A. Ganfield, President of Carroll College in Waukesha, Wisconsin, to oppose the Senator in the primary election. Ganfield concentrated his effort on criticizing La Follette's proposal to strip the Supreme Court of its power to invalidate congressional legislation and emphasized the Senator's ties to the Socialist party, which had not even bothered to nominate a candidate to oppose him.[30] The primary results were an overwhelming vindication of the incumbent. La Follette carried 70 of Wisconsin's 71 counties and received 362,445 votes to Ganfield's 139,327.[31] Virtually all of the Senator's state-wide slate, including Governor Blaine, were victorious. The primary proved that La Follette was still the boss of the Wisconsin Republican party, rather than Senator Lenroot, as the administration had hoped.

The primary victory produced renewed rumblings concerning a La Follette Presidential bid in 1924. The success of Progressive challengers in ousting conservative Republican Senators in North Dakota and Iowa suggested that La Follette's appeal extended beyond the borders of Wisconsin. Although La Follette still had to defeat the Democratic candidate, Mrs. Jessie Jack Hooper, to retain his Senate seat, it was obvious he was more acutely interested in increasing his standing as a national political power. Thus he focused his energies on helping the Progressive challenger, Dr. Henrik Shipstead, defeat the incumbent Old Guard Republican in Minnesota, Senator Frank B. Kellogg.

La Follette bore a special animus towards Kellogg, in part because it was the Minnesota Senator who in 1917 had introduced the resolution of his state's Public Safety Committee in the Senate, calling for La Follette's expulsion. Another reminder of his wartime ordeal was brought home to La Follette on November 1, 1922, when the Minnesota National Guard denied him use of its armory in Mankato to speak on behalf of Shipstead.[32] When La Follette got his chance to address an overflow crowd of 12,500 in

---

[30]*NYT*, September 3, 1922, 4:2.

[31]*Robert M. La Follette*, Vol. II, p. 1061.

[32]*NYT*, November 2, 1922, 21:5.

St. Paul three days later, he failed to restrain his personal feelings towards Kellogg.

The Minnesota Senator walked with a pronounced stoop, which led La Follette to exclaim:

> God Almighty through nature writes men's characters on their faces and in their forms. Your Senator has bowed obsequiously to wealth and to corporations' orders and to his masters until God Almighty has given him a hump on his back—crouching, cringing, un-American, unmanly. . . .[33]

Fola La Follette, in writing her father's biography, characterized the attack on Kellogg as "unworthy and out of character" and states that her mother was very upset by it. While the meanness of the remark may have been unusual, one has to regard it as characteristic of the manner in which La Follette conducted himself as a United States Senator. Legislators generally are careful to keep the lines of communication open with their political opponents—knowing they may need the future assistance of a colleague. La Follette, however, made no attempt to avoid creating personal animosity with those with whom he disagreed.

Senator Kellogg appealed to Minnesota Democrats to vote for him lest La Follette's candidate win. He noted that he had supported President Wilson during the war, and the Wisconsin Senator had not. La Follette's Democratic opponent in Wisconsin, although given no chance of beating him, also asked the voters to remember the Senator's opposition to the war. In Milwaukee, a few days before the election, Mrs. Hooper stated:

> I have no quarrel with him for voting against the war, but once we were in, it was for him, under his solemn oath, to resign as a Senator of the United States or give every ounce of his ability to his country. La Follette failed to do either one. He is going around saying we went into the war for money. Just think of

---

[33]*Robert M. La Follette*, Vol. II, p. 1063.

it—we Americans sent our own flesh and blood to be killed for money. Well it isn't true. Now he is calling us boobs. . . .[34]

At the Senator's death, the *Milwaukee Journal* observed that "[i]t is probable that had his term expired in 1918 he could not have been re-elected. . . ."[35] However, in politics, timing is everything. La Follette won the general election by a margin of 279,000 to 78,000.

In Minnesota, Shipstead upset Kellogg, and the end result of the 1922 election was a considerable narrowing of the Republican majority in Congress. The Senate had 52 Republicans, 43 Democrats, and Shipstead, elected under the banner of the Farm-Labor party. In the House, there were 220 Republicans, 212 Democrats, and three others (including the Socialist Victor Berger of Milwaukee).

The smaller GOP majority meant that the progressive Republicans, La Follette, Norris and Howell of Nebraska, Brookhart of Iowa, Hiram Johnson of California, and Frazier of North Dakota, held the balance of power in the Senate. The progressive Republican Representatives, including the Wisconsin Congressmen and Fiorello H. La Guardia of New York, held a similar position in the House. Although not relevant to La Follette's increasingly important position in Congress, the results of the Senatorial race in Ohio also gave La Follette considerable satisfaction. His tormentor from the war years, Atlee Pomerene, lost his seat by 45,000 votes.[36]

Soon after the election, La Follette called for a progressive conference in Washington, D.C. Some speculated that the conference was the first step towards the formation of a third party for 1924 to include La Follette and William Jennings Bryan.[37] The replacement of the Democratic party with one of a more left-wing orientation did not seem far fetched in view

---

[34]*Milwaukee Sentinel*, November 1, 1922, 4:2.

[35]*Milwaukee Journal*, June 18, 1925, 8:1.

[36]*NYT*, November 9, 1922, 1:5.

[37]*NYT*, November 15, 1922, 1:8; November 19, 1922, 1:1.

of events in England. There the Liberal party was eclipsed by the Labor party, which gained control of the government in 1922, under Ramsay MacDonald. MacDonald, like La Follette, was his country's most notorious dissenter from the policies of his government during World War I. To his detractors, La Follette's increasing importance, boded only ill. *The New York Times* observed,

> The immediate intention of Senator La Follette is plainly to make all the trouble he can in Congress.[38]

The progressive conference met in Washington in early December 1922. It adopted resolutions calling for the extension of the direct primary to the selection of the President and Vice-President, and called for the abolition of the Electoral College. The progressives also called for an effective Federal Corrupt Practices Act. The most controversial portion of the conference was an attack on the federal judiciary by Samuel Gompers, President of the AF of L.[39]

A few days later, a special session of the Senate convened to consider President Harding's nomination of Pierce Butler, a corporate lawyer from St. Paul, Minnesota, to the United States Supreme Court. The La Follette-led progressives scored a short-lived victory in preventing quick confirmation of the appointment. However, Butler was ultimately confirmed by a vote of 61-8. *The New York Times* charged that La Follette's real target was Attorney General Harry Daugherty, the President's oldest and closest adviser, whom the *Times* said La Follette wanted to impeach for purely political reasons.[40]

In January 1923, the Senate by a vote of 57-6, passed a resolution calling for the withdrawal of American troops stationed in the German Rhineland, where a small contingent had shared occupation

---

[38]*NYT,* November 20, 1922, 16:1.

[39]*NYT,* December 3, 1922, 1:8.

[40]*NYT,* December 5, 1922, 1:7; December 5, 1922, 18:1, December 22, 1922, 11:1.

responsibilities with the French and British. The resolution was an indication of a gradual change in public opinion towards the recent war. La Follette's view, that the war involved European jealousies from which America should have stayed clear, was gaining acceptance. In the same month, the French government invaded the Ruhr Valley to compel German payment of war reparations. In England, as well in America, many were losing sympathy with the French desire to keep Germany weak and impoverished.[41]

An indication of the Senator's rehabilitation on the war issue was a resolution introduced into the Wisconsin State Senate by Henry A. Huber, the majority leader, calling for the burning of the wartime University of Wisconsin faculty resolution condemning La Follette. The move to burn the anti-La Follette resolution was squelched by the Senator who wrote Huber that although he appreciated the gesture, he did not want the document destroyed:

> I stated many times from the public platform in Wisconsin during the recent campaign that I would not exchange my record on the war with any man in the United States. History alone can judge impartially. So far as I am concerned, I am content that this document shall remain as physical evidence of the hysteria attendant upon the war.[42]

Although the Wisconsin legislature did not call for the destruction of the resolution, which had been signed by 450 faculty members, it formally condemned the action by a vote of 17-12 in the Senate and 82-11 in the Assembly.[43] A letter to the editors of *The New York Times* published on March 17, charged that the action of the legislature was a threat to academic freedom. William Stearns Davis warned that every professor at

---

[41]*NYT,* January 7, 1923, 2:2; January 12, 1923.

[42]*NYT,* January 20, 1923, 4:5; February 15, 1923, 14:2; March 7, 1923, 8:2.

[43]*NYT,* March 8, 1923, 3:4; March 9, 1923; 9:2.

the University of Wisconsin would feel that his salary, promotion, and tenure would be in jeopardy if he expressed any opinion "adverse to the dominant La Follette-radical regime."[44]

In April, President Harding gave a speech favoring American participation in the World Court. La Follette charged that this was part of an effort by international bankers to commit the United States to European political controversies. In responding to the President the Senator declared:

> [T]he American people will instinctively shun all entanglements in foreign affairs that will lead them inevitably into another European War. [T]here is nothing that the United States can do that will solve the European situation until the Treaty of Versailles is obliterated and the peoples of Europe cast hatred, malice, and revenge from their minds and hearts, abandon ruinous reparation demands, repudiate their imperialistic governments and themselves rebuild the shattered structure of Western civilization.
>
> We have already set Europe a good example by refusing to ratify the Treaty of Versailles. . . .[45]

An unexpected opportunity for La Follette to test his popularity against that of the Harding administration arose in May 1923, when Minnesota Senator Knute Nelson died. La Follette mailed an appeal for the election of Magnus Johnson, the Farm-Labor candidate to 400,000 Minnesota voters. The regular Republican candidate, Governor Preuss tried to distance himself from the administration due to overwhelming unpopularity of the Republican tariff amongst Minnesota farmers. Johnson defeated Preuss 259,500–184,900, causing *The New York Times*

---

[44]*NYT,* March 17, 1923, 12:6.

[45]*NYT*, April 26, 1923, 2:1.

to exclaim in a front page headline, "WASHINGTON JARRED BY MINNESOTA VOTE."[46] Senator La Follette publicly proclaimed that the Johnson victory was a indication of a nation-wide antipathy to monopoly power and not just a sectional peculiarity. Senator George Moses, head of the Republican Senatorial Campaign Committee said the election result was due to low wheat prices. He predicted that the political ramifications of the agricultural depression were spreading and would lead to a bid by La Follette for the Republican Presidential nomination. Moses predicted that La Follette would come to the Republican convention in 1924 with 102 delegates committed to him.[47]

In August, the Wisconsin Senator sailed abroad for the first time in his life. Along with several other Senators, La Follette embarked upon a visit to Europe. Several days out to sea, he learned that President Harding died suddenly on the West Coast. He wired a statement home that, "although . . . we seldom agreed upon questions of major importance, he ever accorded to me that cordiality of personal relationship indicative of his fair and friendly spirit . . . ."[48]

During his trip to Europe, La Follette made a visit to Soviet Russia, which at that time had no diplomatic relations with the United States. Arriving in the company of the muckraking journalist, Lincoln Steffens and the sculptor, Jo Davidson, the Senator indicated an intention to stay in Russia for several weeks. Unexpectedly, he left for Warsaw, Poland, after only four days. Although it is not clear what caused him to cut his visit short, from his antipathy expressed towards American Communists, one can surmise that the Senator was not completely pleased with what he saw in Moscow.

Returning home in early November, La Follette said the United States should help alleviate starvation in Germany. He warned that unless America helped save the Weimar Republic, it would be replaced by

---

[46]*NYT,* July 18, 1923, 1:1.

[47]*NYT,* July 18, 1923, 2:4; July 21, 1923, 3:1.

[48]*NYT,* August 5, 1923, 3:5.

Communism or anarchy. The very week of the Senator's return, a thirty-four-year-old German war veteran led a band of his followers, described as "Bavarian fascists" by *The New York Times*, in an effort to seize control of the government of Bavaria. The group planned then to march on Berlin. Aided by Erich Ludendorff, the virtual military dictator of Germany during the war, Adolph Hitler captured the imagination of a sizeable and growing segment of the German population. He attacked the Treaty of Versailles, the humiliation of Germany by the French occupation of the Ruhr, and blamed all Germany's problems on the Jews and others whom he deemed to be the German people's domestic enemies. On November 9, 1923, Hitler failed in his bid for power and nearly lost his life. Less than ten years later, he would be appointed Reich Chancellor by Paul von Hindenburg, Ludendorff's nominal wartime boss, and would indeed undo the Versailles Treaty.

One of the things that facilitated Hitler's rise to power was a feeling among many in Germany and abroad that Germany had been seriously wronged in the post-war treaty. In May 1924, the Socialist Congressman Victor Berger introduced a resolution in the U. S. House of Representatives calling on the United States to initiate a conference to revise the Versailles Treaty. Berger claimed, as many in Germany came to believe, that President Wilson had tricked the Germans into agreeing to the armistice by promising that his Fourteen Points would be the basis of the post-war peace treaty.[49]

---

[49]*NYT*, May 12, 1924, 19:3.

John Sharp Williams lambastes La Follette

The Big Four at Versailles: Lloyd George, Orlando, Clemenceau, and Wilson.

There remains, then, the Wisconsin Red, with his pockets stuffed with Soviet gold. I shall vote for him unhesitatingly, and for the plain reason: he is the best man running, **as a man**. There is no ring in his nose. Nobody owns him. Nobody bosses him. Nobody even advises him. Right or wrong, he has stood on his own bottom, firmly and resolutely, since the day he was first heard of in politics, battling for his ideas in good weather and bad, facing great odds gladly, going against his followers as well as with his followers, taking his own line always and sticking to it with superb courage and resolution.

Suppose all Americans were like La Follette? What a country it would be! No more depressing goose-stepping. No more gorillas in hysterical herds. No more trimming and trembling. Does it matter what his ideas are? Personally, I am against four-fifths of them, but what are the odds? There are, at worst, better than the ignominiuous platitutdes of Coolidge. They are better than the evasions of Davis...

The older I grow the less I esteem mere ideas. In politics, particularly, they are transient and unimportant...There are only men who have character and men who lack it. La Follette has it. There is no shaking or alarming him. He is devoid of caution, policy, timidity, baseness—all the immemorial qualities of the politician. He is tremendous when he is right and he is even more tremendous when he is wrong...

H. L. Mencken, *The Voter's Dilemma*, November 3, 1924, quoted in Mencken, *A Carnival of Buncombe*, pp. 116-17, and Murray Kempton, *Rebellions, perversities, and main events*, p. 82.

130

CHAPTER 7
Third Party Candidate, 1924

In the spring of 1924, speculation commenced regarding Senator La Follette's strategy for the coming Presidential election. In January, *The New York Times* predicted that he would not run as a third party candidate because he would be more influential boring from within the Republican party.[1] In March 1924, the Socialist Norman Thomas predicted a serious third party presidential effort and said that La Follette was the most logical candidate.[2]

Although nobody believed that La Follette could win enough electoral votes to become President, his supporters and his detractors did think it was possible for him to throw the Presidential election into the House of Representatives. In the House, he could possibly emerge as President, or otherwise force the selection of a President acceptable to Progressives. The scenario was that La Follette would get enough electoral votes to prevent either President Coolidge or the Democratic candidate from getting a majority of the electoral votes.

The Constitution mandates that if no candidate has a majority of the electoral votes, the President is selected by the House of Representatives, with each state getting one vote. Only twice in American history has this happened; in 1801 Thomas Jefferson was elected President by the House because he and his running mate, Aaron Burr, had an identical number of votes. In 1825, John Quincy Adams was also elected by the House.

In 1924, 23 of the 48 state Congressional delegations were Republican, which included several such as Wisconsin's on which President Coolidge could not necessarily depend for support. Twenty delegations were Democratic, and five were evenly divided. Thus, it was unlikely that

---

[1]*NYT*, January 18, 1924, 16:1.

[2]*Ibid.*, March 2, 1924, IX, 5:4.

if the 1924 Presidential election were thrown into the House that either the Democratic or Republican candidate would have enough support to win.[3]

Another scenario was that no candidate could get a majority in the House but that the Senate, which picks the Vice-President in the event of gridlock in the electoral college, could agree on a candidate. If the Senate selected a Vice-President and no President was picked by the House by March 4, 1925, the Senate's selection would become President.

In May, W.T. Raleigh, a very wealthy Chicagoan, who was La Follette's chief financial backer and chairman of the La Follette for President Committee, warned that the Senator would run if the Republicans and Democrats nominated reactionary candidates. A few days later, the Senator was hinting that he might run and at the same time making it clear that he would not welcome support from American Communists. He condemned the Farm-Labor party for allowing the Communists to participate in their national convention and warned that the Communists were trying to use the Progressive movement for their own ends.[4]

The Conference for Progressive Political Action convened a national convention in Cleveland, Ohio, in July for purposes of nominating a Presidential candidate. Robert La Follette, Jr., appeared before the convention in which he announced his father's willingness to run. On July 5, 1924, the convention nominated La Follette by acclamation to run against President Coolidge and John W. Davis, who was nominated at the Democratic convention on the 103rd ballot. Davis was a Wall Street lawyer who had served as U.S. Ambassador to England and Solicitor General of the United States.

The New York Times greeted La Follette's nomination with an editorial entitled, "Not Progressive, Destructive." *The Times* concluded:

> His program includes projects, that if they could be carried out, would sweepingly change American policy. The subversion of

---

[3]*NYT,* May 4, 1924, IX, page 1, "Third Party Could Deadlock Election."

[4]*Ibid.,* May 29, 1924, 1:6.

the Supreme Court by Congress, the shackling of other Federal courts for the supposed benefit of the labor unions, would be a destructive change.[5]

One who saw the nomination differently was William Allen White, a life-long Republican and editor of the Emporia (Kansas) *Gazette:*

> For thirty years his name has been growing famous in American politics—and always it has stood for one thing—courageous, constructive, ultra-liberalism. . . . La Follette has ever been a lone fighter. Compromise is not in his lexicon. . . . His convention in Cleveland, in July, was hardly a convention at all. It was a tribute; a splendid tribute to a brave man whose wisdom for thirty active, successful years in American politics has been vindicated by time more often than that of any other contemporary statesman. He is a man of the highest personal character. Personally, he is incorruptible. Politically, he is immovable in his determination to battle in a finish fight for what he deems a just and righteous cause. His intellectual processes are strong and sound. In no personal quality of heart or mind is either of his adversaries his superior. Birth, heredity, environment, have made him a crusader. He loves a long trek—the lone trail.[6]

Representatives of the three major candidates gave contrasting views as to significance of the La Follette campaign. Cordell Hull, Chairman of the Democratic National Committee (later Secretary of State under FDR) predicted that La Follette would hurt President Coolidge and help Davis. The President's camp said that La Follette would draw the radical vote

---

[5]*NYT,* July 12, 1924, 8:1.

[6]White, *The Citizen's Business,* p. 122.

that would otherwise go to Davis, thereby helping Coolidge.[7] J. A. Hopkins, a La Follette campaign official, predicted that the Senator would draw heavily from the 55% of the electorate that didn't vote in 1920.[8]

La Follette gathered support from liberal luminaries across the country. Among his supporters were Congressman Fiorello H. La Guardia, Amos Pinchot, the conservationist, Helen Keller, and Oswald Garrison Villard, editor of *The Nation*, and grandson of the abolitionist, William Lloyd Garrison. While eschewing Communist support, La Follette welcomed the backing of American Socialists. A ringing endorsement of the Senator's candidacy came from Eugene V. Debs, the Socialist leader who had run for President himself before serving several years in prison for speaking against the draft laws. Debs told his followers:

> Though he is not a Socialist, we need not blush or apologize to give our support to Robert La Follette in the live-giving and hope-inspiring struggle of the present hour. All his life he has stood up like a man for the right, according to his light; he has been shamefully maligned, ostracized and persecuted by the predatory powers of the plutocracy, yet his bitterest foe has never dared to question his personal integrity or his political rectitude.[9]

As La Follette's running mate, the Progressives nominated 42-year-old Senator Burton K. Wheeler of Montana. A Democrat, Wheeler had refused to support John W. Davis because of his Wall Street connections. The La Follette campaign officially adopted the name "Progressive" and chose the Liberty Bell as its symbol. The director of publicity for the campaign was Dr. Ernest H. Gruening, who in 1964 was one of two United

---

[7]*NYT,* July 18, 1924, 3:2, 4:2.

[8]*NYT,* August 5, 1924, 2:7.

[9]*NYT,* July 17, 1924, 3:2.

134

States Senators to vote against the Tonkin Gulf resolution that allowed President Johnson to commit U.S. forces to major warfare in Vietnam.

In the late summer, all three Presidential candidates came under pressure to take a stand on the Ku Klux Klan, which had become increasingly popular in the South and mid-West[10]. Davis, whose party depended most on the white Southern vote was in the most difficult position. If he condemned the Klan, he would alienate white Protestant supporters. If he failed to condemn the Klan, he would alienate the Roman Catholic groups that constituted much of his party's constituency in the North. The best the candidate could do was announce that he had never been and would never be a member of the KKK.

La Follette also risked losing the support of poor white farmers, whose votes he counted on, if he denounced the Klan. On August 5, 1924, the Senator released a letter to a prominent supporter, Robert P. Scripps, head of the Scripps newspaper chain, denouncing the Klan. La Follette cited a famous Abraham Lincoln letter in which Lincoln declared that if the Know-Nothings gained control of the United States, he would prefer to move to Russia, where despotism could be taken pure—without hypocrisy.

In September, President Coolidge attacked La Follette's views on the Supreme Court. The Senator's close friend, Gilbert Roe, who represented him before the Senate in 1917-1918 responded. Roe, who had very respectable credentials as a legal scholar, said the Constitution never gave the Court the power to invalidate the acts of Congress; the Court had usurped this power. The Court, said Roe, was claiming power that was generally asserted by royalty—without any more justification.[11]

The Coolidge campaign garnered a statement from 48 supporters of Theodore Roosevelt's 1912 candidacy as a Progressive, to denounce La Follette. Included among the signatories was James Garfield, President

---

[10]The Klan virtually controlled the State of Indiana during the early 1920s and was powerful enough that Hugo Black, later one of the greatest civil libertarians to sit on the United States Supreme Court, joined the Klan in Alabama to advance his political career.

[11]*NYT,* September 9, 1924, 6:1.

Garfield's son, who had been TR's Interior Secretary. Gilbert Roe responded by pointing out that Roosevelt's 1912 platform was in many ways more radical than La Follette's. It had called for overturning judicial decisions by referendum and recall of federal judges by popular vote.[12]

The Democratic strategy was to court La Follette voters and avoid criticizing the Senator. Franklin D. Roosevelt, returning to politics after his bout with polio, predicted that as the election drew nearer more and more voters would realize that a vote for the Senator would be wasted and that a vote for Coolidge would be a vote for governmental deadlock. Coolidge, said FDR, would be unable to govern effectively given the power of the Congressional coalition of Democrats and Progressive Republicans.[13]

As is so often the case in American Presidential elections, the sharpest attacks on La Follette came not from President Coolidge, but from his surrogates. The Republican Vice-Presidential candidate, Charles G. Dawes, in a Milwaukee speech, called the Senator "a master demagogue," citing his attack on the Supreme Court and his ties with the American Socialists.[14]

The Democratic strategy, however, was to treat La Follette with kid gloves. They hoped to avoid alienating the Senator's supporters—with the expectation that many of La Follette's supporters would ultimately vote for Davis when they realized that only the Democrat had a chance of defeating the President. In addressing La Follette's proposals regarding the Supreme Court, for example, Davis said he disagreed with the Progressive candidate, but thought that the Coolidge camp was trying to scare the voters with the notion that La Follette's ideas were Communist inspired.

Davis said the Wisconsin Senator's ideas were more akin to the British concept of parliamentary supremacy than any sort of Bolshevik concept. While in his view American constitutional theory was superior to the English, Davis said the Republican attacks on La Follette were similar

---

[12]*NYT,* September 16, 1924, 3:3.

[13]*NYT,* September 19, 1924, 3:1.

[14]*NYT,* September 12, 1924, 1:6.

to their habit of "waving the bloody shirt" after the Civil War to inflame the electorate.[15]

Not all of La Follette's supporters were quite so willing to treat the Democrats with reciprocal good will. Speaking from the same platform as the Senator at Madison Square Garden in New York, a noted suffragette, Harriet Stanton Blatch, reminded her 14,000 listeners:

> If we accuse Daugherty [Harding's Attorney-General], we do not forget Palmer [Wilson's Attorney-General who organized extra-legal raids against suspected radicals]. Daugherty robbed us of our property, but Palmer robbed us of self-respect and our liberty. Palmer turned this nation into nation of cowards.[16]

The entire La Follette family took to the campaign trail. The Senator's wife, Belle Case La Follette, was one of the first female law school graduates in the United States. Although she generally stayed in the background during his political career, she said what she thought while campaigning—without worrying about whether she and her husband were in complete agreement. At a rally in Maryland, Mrs. La Follette went far beyond the positions stated by the Senator in criticizing the growth of American military spending. She proclaimed:

> So long as control by big business in government continues, the pressure for the biggest army and navy will go on. If we continue our present military and naval policy, approved by both Democratic and Republican administrations, we shall be the most militarized nation in the world.[17]

---

[15]*NYT,* September 28, 1924, 1:7. The "bloody shirt" was a tactic employed by the Republicans after the Civil War to identify the Democratic party with acts of violence against freed slaves and white Republicans in the South.

[16]*NYT,* September 19, 1924, 2:1.

[17]*NYT,* September 29, 1924, 1:7.

On the issue of the morality of war itself, Mrs. La Follette went out of her way to distance her views from those of her husband:

> I am a pacifist. I cannot say that Mr. La Follette is one. He thinks there may be a supreme principle for which, under extraordinary circumstances, men must fight as a last resort.[18]

In early October, La Follette gained the support of Harold Ickes, TR's Illinois campaign manager in 1912 and the future Secretary of the Interior under FDR. The Republicans trotted out Teddy Roosevelt's sister, Corinne Roosevelt Robinson, to denounce La Follette as an enemy of her late brother—which, of course, he was—particularly during the War. The Davis camp gained an endorsement from the famous muckraking journalist, Ida Tarbell, who said she couldn't vote for La Follette because he had spent his political life in the Republican party, the party of protective tariffs. La Follette had last supported a protective tariff in 1890. More significant was the fact that William Jennings Bryan was urging his supporters to vote for Davis on the grounds that only the Democrat had a real chance to defeat President Coolidge. To win Bryan supporters, the Democrats had nominated his brother, then Governor of Nebraska, for Vice-President.[19]

Senator La Follette picked up support from a number of influential black Americans. Most notable of these was W.E.B. Dubois, editor of *The Crisis*, the official organ of the NAACP, and the best-known advocate of black civil rights. Dubois said blacks should vote for La Follette because he had condemned the KKK, opposed U.S. imperialism in Haiti, and opposed all forms of racial discrimination.[20]

Bishop John Hurst, a black Methodist leader, urged support for La Follette as well. Hurst cited President Coolidge's silence with regard to the Klan and what he saw as the Republicans' failure to follow through on any

---

[18]*Ibid.*

[19]*NYT,* October 3, 1924, 7:1; 3:4; October 5, X 8:2; October 6, 6:2.

[20]*NYT,* October 21, 1924, 6:5.

of the promises made to blacks. While candidate Davis had denounced the Klan, Hurst said the Democrats were still the party of the KKK and Jim Crow (legally enforced segregation).[21]

La Follette's attitude towards the Jews became an issue when Louis Marshall, a prominent Jewish attorney and supporter of President Coolidge, accused the Senator of aiding in the circulation of documents blaming the start of World War I on Jewish bankers.[22] Gilbert Roe answered Marshall by explaining that La Follette had put certain material in the *Congressional Record* as a favor to Senator Morris Sheppard of Texas. Roe said the Wisconsin Senator had not read the material and was unaware of the anti-Semitic nature of an article entitled, "Justice for Hungary." The Senator, Roe said, repudiated the document and withdrew his mailing privileges from it, as soon as he was apprised of its contents.[23]

La Follette reiterated the explanation given by Roe and reminded Jewish voters that *he* had led the fight for confirmation of the first Jewish Supreme Court Justice, Louis D. Brandeis, and had favored severing U.S. diplomatic relations with Czarist Russia at the time of its government-sponsored pogroms.[24] Among the Senator's prominent Jewish supporters were Rabbi Abba Hillel Silver of Cleveland, Mrs. Brandeis, and Morris Hillquit, a Jewish Socialist leader. Mrs. Brandeis noted that despite all the talk about La Follette's radicalism, virtually all the reforms he advocated had ultimately been enacted into law.[25]

As La Follette travelled around the country, he repeatedly harkened back to World War I and what he saw as its legacy. Two of his more

---

[21]*NYT*, October 7, 1924, 7:2. Indeed, in the 1950s John W. Davis would conclude his legal career defending school segregation before the United States Supreme Court as lead counsel for the State of South Carolina.

[22]*NYT*, October 29, 1924, 2:7.

[23]*NYT* October 30, 1924. Senator Sheppard also disclaimed knowledge of the character of the article.

[24]*NYT*, November 1, 1924, II, 3:7.

[25]*Ibid.*, October 15, 1924, 6:1.

significant speeches in this regard were given in October in Cincinnati and St. Louis, cities with substantial German-American populations.

On October 10, 1924, the Progressive candidate spoke to 4,000 listeners inside Cincinnati's Music Hall, with 3,000 more people listening to him outside over a public address system. La Follette told the crowd:

> I am convinced that the Great War in Europe was not a war of unprovoked aggression by one nation. It was a war which had its birth in secret diplomacy, in national fears kept alive by military castes and most of all by private munitions makers and a capitalistic press in all the great powers. . . .
>
> * * *
>
> The treaty of Versailles . . . was a treaty of financial imperialists, of exploiters, of bankers, of oil monopolists. . . .

La Follette concluded by laying the blame for all the international tension on what he termed "financial imperialism."[26]

The speech got very mixed reviews from the Cincinnati press. *The Cincinnati Post*, owned by La Follette admirer, Robert Scripps, said that the crowd:

> [H]eard from the candidate a speech that was devoid of the usual political hokum. It was a straight forward plea and a promise to end wars by taking the profit out of them. It was based on a perfectly workable foreign policy proposed by the Progressive leader. No bluster. No bunk. Just truth and high idealism.[27]

A few weeks later, *The Post* endorsed, at least implicitly, the La Follette candidacy. After lending its support to his desire to give Congress

---

[26]*The Cincinnati Post*, October 11, 1924, 5.

[27]*Ibid.*, 4:1.

the power to override Supreme Court decisions,[28] the paper proclaimed on the day before the election:

> Senator La Follette proposes a housecleaning at Washington that will sweep out special privilege and restore the government to the people.
>
> If the people want their government back, here is their chance.[29]

The other major newspapers in the city saw the speech very differently. Although inhabited by many of German descent, Cincinnati was (and is) very conservative, and was the hometown of ex-President Taft, then the Chief Justice of the U.S. Supreme Court—a prime target of La Follette's critique of the country's political system.

The Cincinnati Enquirer gave top billing to the World Series victory of the Washington Senators rather than the La Follette speech. The paper did report that the Senator denied that he was a pacifist and that he took President Wilson to task for getting America involved in the European War almost immediately after being re-elected for keeping us out of the conflict.[30] In an editorial entitled "The Liberty Bell Dance," *The Enquirer* let its readers know what it really thought of the Senator:

> One who incites class against class, who foments discontent, who luxuriates in seasons of depression and disaster—one who assails traditional guarantees which affect the property and lives of citizens—one who has gathered unto his cause the rag-tag of Socialism throughout our coasts, and who still has the

---

[28]*Ibid.,* October 29, 1924, 4:1.

[29]*Ibid.,* November 3, 1924.

[30]*The Cincinnati Enquirer,* October 11, 1924, 1:2.

effrontery to write his name under the sacrosanct symbol of the Liberty Bell. . . ."[31]

The Cincinnati Times-Star virtually ignored the candidate's speech except to deliver a broadside against him in its editorial pages two days afterwards:

> La Follette was not making an exposition of foreign policy and not talking in behalf of peace at all. . . . [H]is address was solely intended to harvest the dissatisfaction of those who believe that America should have had no part in the World War. To do this he did not hesitate at two ugly things. The first was to imply that there was nothing of idealism or patriotism or even the inevitabilities of a policy of self-defense in America's drawing of the sword. The second was to withhold a single word of commendation from the programme—call it the Dawes plan, or call it what you please—under which the former "allied and associated powers" and Germany have at last come together in a sincere and vastly hopeful effort to achieve the common good.[32]

---

[31]*Ibid.,* October 12, 1924, 6:1.

[32]*The Cincinnati Times-Star*, October 13, 1924, 6:1. The Dawes plan, named after the Republican Vice-Presidential candidate, was an effort by American, British, and German bankers to make payment of the war reparations more bearable for the Germans. By 1925 the German government had brought inflation under control and the relief brought by the Dawes plan seemed to be working in getting Germany back on its feet, economically. However, when the depression hit Germany in 1929 all the wounds inflicted by the Versailles Treaty were re-opened. German grievances regarding their mistreatment at Versailles, real and imagined, coupled with economic distress, brought the Nazis, a lunatic fringe in 1928, to power in an amazingly short period.

In St. Louis, another city with a significant German-American population, La Follette again raised the war issue:

> When war was declared in Europe . . . President Wilson declared for absolute neutrality—neutrality in thought, word and deed. If this doctrine had been adhered to we would never have been drawn into war.

Later, the Senator placed responsibility for the war squarely on the influence of J.P. Morgan:

> I am convinced . . . that we abandoned our foreign policy through the influence of J.P. Morgan & Co., the fiscal agent of the British Empire, who in the early spring of 1917, turned loose the press and the agencies of propaganda to drive us into war to save his billions.[33]

The delicts of Woodrow Wilson were more than of historical interest to the Senator. He proclaimed that the departure from traditional [and impliedly, sound] U. S. foreign policy had begun under his friend, McKinley, had continued under Roosevelt and Taft, and was "completely abandoned by Wilson, Harding and Coolidge."[34]

With the election only weeks away, estimates regarding the impact of the La Follette campaign varied greatly. John W. Davis predicted that the Progressive would carry six to eight states.[35] Democratic Senator Carter Glass, on the other hand, said that La Follette had no chance of winning and that the Republicans were trying to create hysteria over the La Follette court proposals.[36]

---

[33]*Literary Digest,* November 1, 1924, 14.

[34]*NYT,* October 15, 1924, 9:1.

[35]*NYT,* October 20, 1924, 1:6.

[36]*NYT,* October 28, 1924, 4:2.

The Literary Digest in its rather unscientific poll predicted a huge Coolidge victory. The Democrats were quick to point out that the magazine predicted a Hughes victory in 1916.[37] As the campaign neared its conclusion, prominent Democrats, such as William G. McAdoo, Wilson's son-in-law and former Treasury Secretary, Colonel Edward House, Wilson's principal advisor, continued to avoid criticism of La Follette. Ambassador Davis seems hardly to have been much of an issue either. The only spirited exchanges in the campaign were between the La Follette and Coolidge camps.

Martin Littleton, a prominent Coolidge supporter, virtually accused La Follette of being an agent of the Soviet Union.[38] On the other hand, Senator La Follette was hardly more restrained when he talked about the President. In Pittsburgh, he described Treasury Secretary Mellon, who was a resident of that city and one of the richest men in the country, as the "real President of the United States," thus implying that Coolidge was merely a puppet of the great financiers.[39] The Senator closed his campaign with a huge rally in Cleveland. An estimated 25,000 people heard his address in a city he actually carried.

On November 4, 1924, the people went to the polls and, contrary to the hopes of La Follette and his supporters, effectively drew an end to the "Progressive era." Many on the left believed that if the voters only had a clear choice, they would end government by the business interests. Instead, the voters, given a clear choice, elected President Coolidge by a huge margin. It is true that the Republican party spent far more money than the Democrats, who spent much more than the Progressives. However, La Follette's candidacy did receive enough publicity that if the American people really wanted the wholesale change he advocated, they would have elected him.

---

[37]*NYT*, October 20, 1924, 2:5. Although *The Digest* poll was correct in 1924, it predicted a landslide victory for Republican Alfred Landon against Franklin D. Roosevelt in 1936.

[38]*NYT*, October 23, 1924, 1:6.

[39]*NYT*, November 1, 1924, 3:1.

The President ended up with 382 electoral votes and 54% of the popular vote. Davis received 136 electoral votes and only 29% of the popular vote. La Follette carried only Wisconsin and its 13 electoral votes and received 16% of the popular vote (4.8 million out of 28.9 million)

La Follette's percentage of the popular vote was the best showing by any third party candidate in this century, other than Teddy Roosevelt, who was an ex-President when he ran in 1912—until Ross Perot in 1992. However, the campaign was a great disappointment. The Senator's reaction to the drubbing was far from gracious. Without any real evidence for his charges, he claimed that the voters felt threatened by the money thrown into the campaign by the Republicans, and that workers were threatened with the loss of their jobs and farmers with foreclosure of their mortgages, if Coolidge lost.

The Senator said he was unable to believe that the election was an endorsement of the Harding-Coolidge record, and it seems apparent that there is nothing that could have convinced him otherwise. Instead, he tried to create the myth of some diabolical economic conspiracy.[40]

Others from the campaign took a more sober view. J.A.H. Hopkins attributed the Progressive's poor showing to: 1) making the Supreme Court an issue; and 2) counting on the unions to "deliver" their members. He concluded that the election showed that a lack of class-consciousness in the United States made it impossible to replicate the success of the British Labor party.[41]

Another post-mortem analysis was made by the journalist, Mark Sullivan, in an article entitled "Looking Back on La Follette," in January 1925.[42] Sullivan too saw the La Follette campaign as an effort to replace the Democrats as the liberal party in America. He thought the Progressives failed for several reasons: first, because La Follette had too many issues; second, because big business was not nearly as suspect as it

---

[40]*NYT,* November 24, 1924, 3:1.

[41]*NYT,* January 2, 1925, 6:1.

[42]*World's Work,* 49:324 (January 31, 1925).

had been in the first decade of the twentieth century. The war, Sullivan thought, had clothed big business with greater respectability. Finally, although he saw La Follette as the only conceivable leader of a new party, Sullivan thought he conveyed an emotional excitability, which hurt him with the voters when contrasted with the staid persona of his adversaries—particularly those on the Supreme Court.

The poor showing of the Progressive ticket greatly damaged La Follette's political power in the Senate. The Old Guard Republicans felt that the election results would enable them to finally ride the Senator out of the party and strip him of his chairmanship of the Senate Committee on Manufactures.

The Senator kept hammering away at those whom he considered enemies of the common man. In his magazine, he charged that big business had gained control of higher education by making it financially dependent on its support. He cited Columbia University and his long-time enemy, Nicholas Murray Butler, as an example:

> President Butler toadies to all the millionaires who have made or are likely to make large gifts to education by his declaration [in favor of] the future exemption of great wealth from taxation.[43]

Although Senator La Follette's health had been deteriorating for a number of years, he began to decline even more rapidly in early 1925. He absented himself from the Senate and went to Fort Lauderdale, Florida, for an extended period of recuperation. In March the Progressives in the Senate challenged President Coolidge's nomination of Charles B. Warren, who had represented the sugar interests, to be Attorney General. La Follette missed the debate on the nomination, but when the nominee failed to win confirmation on the first try, he traveled back to Washington to prevent a successful second attempt.

The renewed attempt to confirm Warren was defeated by a vote of 46 against the nominee and 39 in favor. The majority included 35 Democrats,

---

[43]*NYT,* January 22, 1925, 23:2.

10 nominal Republicans including La Follette, Borah, Norris, and Hiram Johnson, and Shipstead, the Farm-Labor Senator from Minnesota. The failure of the Coolidge administration to carry the Warren appointment indicated that La Follette was still a force to be reckoned with.

In mid-June, the Senator became ill again, and on June 18, 1925, he died of heart disease, complicated by bronchial asthma and pneumonia. La Follette had turned 70 years old a few days before. The assessments of his career varied widely, but what is noteworthy is that most of the objective assessments of his career, by friend and foe, agreed that La Follette should be judged first and foremost by his stand against American entry into World War I, the aspect of his career that is now most frequently overlooked.

Norman Thomas, an admirer who would become the perennial Socialist candidate for President, said:

> His stand on the War is now glossed over both by his friends and his enemies, but he said what is now recognized as the truth—that it was a struggle between two imperialisms. He was never a pro-German in the strict sense.[44]

The Nation's editor, Oswald Garrison Villard, agreed:

> He did one of the great things in the history of the American people. I refer to his magnificent stand at the time of the declaration of war. How easy it would have been for him to have sided with the majority, as other Senators did.[45]

The editors of *The Milwaukee Journal*, long-time political opponents of La Follette, gave a thoughtful but contrary view:

---

[44]*NYT,* June 25, 1925, 21:5.

[45]*Ibid.*

La Follette, as a young man in the House, had been a regular party man. He had praised the war with Spain, had been a McKinley protectionist. But he came to the Senate as a protester. . . .

On La Follette's war stand, he will be judged by this generation. Not of German blood, often declaring that he was of Huguenot [French Protestant] ancestry . . . his championship of the wishes of those who sympathized with Germany carried the more weight. . . .

What of the estimates of history? . . . The fight against privilege will always go on, and La Follette had a great place in that fight as it was waged in his time. His war attitude will remain hard to condone. . . . [T]he work of the real lover of peace was constructive. It was first to range himself with those who fought to bring victory to their country's arms and then to make out of the furnace of war a better world. La Follette's course began otherwise and he stuck to his beginning, failing to see the one star of hope in a smoke-grimmed and heart-broken world.[46]

A. M. Brayton, publisher of *The Wisconsin State Journal* in Madison, who broke with the Senator over the war, gave an assessment, that although not hostile, pointed to what he saw as La Follette's fatal flaw. "[His] weakness lay in the Senator's inability to extend his hand to those from whom he had parted in displeasure."[47] Brayton believed that once you disagreed with the Senator on anything he felt important, there was something inflexible, unbending, in his nature that made reconciliation impossible.

---

[46]*The Milwaukee Journal,* June 18, 1925, 8:1.

[47]*The Wisconsin State Journal*, June 18, 1925. 1:1.

Regarding La Follette's domestic record, opinions ranged from Victor Berger's view that "he had more constructive legislation to his credit than any other statesman of the present generation,"[48] to the parting shot from *The New York Times*:

> For a man who for so long filled so large a space in our political annals, Senator La Follette left behind a meager record of attainment.[49]

A comprehensive analysis of the Senator's career, entitled "Robert M. La Follette's Place in Our History," was written by Bruce Bliven, an editor of *The New Republic* and appeared in the August 1925 issue of the magazine *Current History*. Bliven had these observations on La Follette's career:

> The charge was often made that he was a demagogue; but if so, he was one with a unique method. The information which he had so laboriously assembled he was in the habit of pouring out upon his constituents inexhaustibly, not to say remorselessly . . . in Wisconsin. . . . [A] whole generation had been educated to listen with interest and often positive pleasure to Bob La Follette's analysis of industrial and economic facts.[50]

Bliven concluded:

> Few men really enjoy the lifelong position of rebel; and when they do, it is usually because they are constitutionally revoltes, who are never happy unless the crowd is against them. La Follette was not of this type. While he was by nature a fighter,

---

[48]*The Milwaukee Journal*, June 19, 1925, 6:1.

[49]*NYT*, June 19, 1925, 18:1.

[50]*The Current History Magazine*, 22:716, 720 (August 1925).

his choice of one side instead of the other in the battle was the result of intellectual determination and moral conviction. You may disagree with him as heartily as you please; most people in the United States at the present time apparently do disagree with him; but you must concede that he was an unquestionably honest man, who fought for nearly half a century, with power and skill, for what he believed to be right.[51]

---

[51]*Ibid.*, at p. 722.

Senator La Follette discusses strategy with Robert M. La Follette, Jr., prior to the Progressive nominating convention in 1924.

The Progressive candidate for President, 1924

CHAPTER 8

The Legacy of Bob La Follette

Bob La Follette's historical legacy, if characterized least favorably, would be the isolationism that led the United States to near disaster in 1941 and 1942. He was succeeded in the U. S. Senate by his oldest son, Robert M. La Follette, Jr., who adhered to virtually identical principles as his father. In the 1930s, the Senator's younger son, Philip F. La Follette, was elected Governor of Wisconsin three times before he turned 40. The two brothers were for a time regarded as the wunderkinds of American politics, and some believed that the Presidency was within the reach of one or the other.

Possibly the most important thing that thwarted the brothers' further political ambitions, if any, was the election of Franklin D. Roosevelt in 1932.[1] FDR, the regular party politician, who had served as Assistant Secretary of the Navy during World War I, and had helped carry Wilson's crusade for the League of Nations to the voters as the Democratic Vice-Presidential candidate in 1920, went "radical" to a great extent after becoming President.

The depression had changed the political landscape dramatically, and the new President was quick to adopt much of the Progressive and Socialist program to combat it. At first, the La Follette brothers were both enthusiastic allies of FDR, but as Philip La Follette's political fortunes faded, he became increasingly disenchanted with Roosevelt, both domestically and on foreign affairs. Defeated in 1938 after a third term as Governor, Phil never held office again and became increasingly reactionary. He was one of the leaders of the America First movement,

---

[1] A fair assessment would be that Bob La Follette, Jr., probably never saw himself as doing anything but continuing his father's battles as U. S. Senator from Wisconsin. Phil La Follette, however, appears to have been a much more ambitious individual.

153

which just before U. S. entry into the Second World War tried to prevent FDR from aiding England in its battle with Hitler.

Once the war began, Philip La Follette volunteered for military service and was a Colonel on the staff of General Douglas MacArthur, an arch-conservative whom La Follette came to greatly admire.[2] The ex-Governor's public career ended as head of a group touting General MacArthur for President in 1948 and 1952.

Bob La Follette, Jr., had a more conventional career than his younger brother. He spent twenty years in the U. S. Senate, during which he was workman-like liberal, dutifully following his father's footsteps. He did not have the penchant for alienating people that distinguished Bob Sr. and was apparently much more popular with his colleagues.

The highlights of Bob, Jr.'s career were a series of hearings held in 1936 for the Senate Civil Liberties Committee, investigating wages and working conditions all over the country. His committee exposed various innovative methods that employers were using to prevent union organizing and to frustrate collective bargaining. For example, he made the public aware of the use of violence and physical intimidation by coal mine operators in Harlan County, Kentucky, to prevent organization by the United Mine Workers.

In foreign affairs, Bob Jr. was also his father's son. He joined with his father's progressive allies, William Borah of Idaho, Burton K. Wheeler of Montana, and Gerald Nye of North Dakota in fighting President Roosevelt's attempts to aid Great Britain in combating Hitler. Both La Follette brothers were close associates of Col. Charles A. Lindbergh (whose father was an anti-war Congressman from Minnesota in 1917) in trying to

---

[2]General MacArthur had strong ties to Wisconsin. His grandfather had settled in Milwaukee, and his father was the teenage commander of the 24th Wisconsin Volunteer Infantry Regiment during the Atlanta campaign.

MacArthur was a very complex man and is probably primarily responsible for Japan's emergence from war and occupation as a stable democracy. However, when one considers his attitude towards the Bonus Marchers in 1932, his views on the relationship between the military and civilian leadership in 1951, and his extreme belligerence towards Communist China, he was a strange bedfellow indeed for a La Follette.

galvanize public opinion in support of neutrality in the war between England and Nazi Germany.

One cannot say for certain that Bob, Sr. would have taken a similar isolationist stance just before Pearl Harbor. One suspects that due to the bitterness he felt about World War I and the Treaty of Versailles, he would have been a hard-core isolationist. It is quite possible that Bob, Sr. would have viewed Hitler's moves to undo the Versailles Treaty as the fulfillment of his predictions and a somewhat deserved comeuppance for England and France.

On the other hand, there were a number of people who believed American intervention in World War I a mistake, who abandoned isolationism when confronted by Hitler. Senator George Norris of Nebraska, who felt just as strongly about the First World War as La Follette, Sr., began to change his views about neutrality dramatically in 1937. Norris was disturbed by Japanese aggression in China, an issue that may have affected La Follette similarly. Norris also came to view the Nazi leadership as constituting a problem totally different from Imperial Germany in 1917.

During the mid 1930s, Congress, under the leadership of the Progressive/isolationist bloc, enacted neutrality legislation aimed at preventing a recurrence of what it felt were the mistakes of 1914-1917. This legislation, for example, provided for an arms embargo to belligerents similar to the one proposed in 1915. One result of this legislation was to place the Loyalist government of Spain at a serious disadvantage in combating the fascist insurgents, who were getting all the arms they needed from the Nazis and Mussolini.

In 1938, Hitler absorbed Austria, and at Munich obtained French and British acquiescence to annex the northern portion of Czechoslovakia (Sudetenland from the German perspective). The latter acquisition had a certain logic because the inhabitants were predominately German. However, Nazi control of this mountainous area deprived the Czech republic of its natural defenses against German attack.

In the spring of 1939, Hitler prepared to occupy the rest of Czechoslovakia. As the German dictator had promised at Munich that the Sudetenland was his last territorial claim in Europe, he proved that

England and France had been ill advised to trust him. President Roosevelt sought to loosen U. S. neutrality laws so that he would be in a position to provide assistance to England and France when war began. Senator Norris supported the President; Bob La Follette, Jr., vehemently opposed him.

Although Norris did vote against FDR's conscription bill in 1940, he voted for lend lease in March 1941, while La Follette, Jr., remained a hard-core isolationist. At the time of this legislation, Britain stood alone against Hitler; France had been conquered and Russia was still digesting eastern Poland, which it obtained as a result of its non-aggression pact with the Nazis. Norris' relations with several of his old allies, particularly Senators Wheeler and Nye, had cooled considerably in light of events in Europe and Norris' support for FDR.[3]

Another convert was the historian/journalist Walter Millis, whose 1935 book *The Road To War* had been the most popular expression of American disenchantment with Woodrow Wilson's great crusade to Europe in 1917. But in 1941 (before Pearl Harbor), Millis observed that isolationists like himself, "assumed that all reasonable men were wishing to eliminate war from the world. Here were men [Hitler and Mussolini] . . . who were deliberately cultivating war as the central framework of society." To those who advocated abandoning Europe to the Nazis and arming a Fortress America, Millis asked, "[W]hy armaments if we are to make peace, and why peace if we need armaments? What are the armaments supposed to be for? What are they to defend—a mere geographical entity, or a way of life, a general system of political and social ideas, which any peace with a victorious Hitler would certainly make impossible?"[4]

In March 1941 Millis authored an article entitled "Notes on the US, 1950," in which he hypothesized the future if opponents of FDR's lend lease proposal (such as the La Follettes) were successful. In Millis' account the

---

[3]Lowitt, *George W. Norris: The Triumph of a Progressive*, p. 258. On domestic issues both Norris and La Follette, Jr. were allies of FDR.

[4]Millis, *The Faith of An American*, 1941.

defeat of lend lease by the U.S. Congress precipitated a Fascist coup that ousted Churchill in England. By blackmailing the Canadians with the fate of their prisoners of war captured in England, the Nazis were able to gain a foothold in North America from which they cleverly pressured the United States towards a Nazi-controlled dictatorship.

Nobody can say whether Robert La Follette, Sr., would have reacted to Hitler and Japanese aggression as did Norris and Millis, or whether he would, as his sons did, assume that FDR was merely repeating the mistakes of Woodrow Wilson. There is some evidence on this issue in a signed editorial which appeared in *La Follette's Weekly* one month before the Senator's death. Many American newspapers were aghast that in 1925 the Germans had elected Paul von Hindenburg, commander of Kaiser's army, as President of the Weimar Republic. La Follette, on the other hand, concluded, "General Hindenburg is pledged to support the constitution of the Republic. What right have we to assume that he will not keep his oath inviolate?"[5]

If the Senator had been alive in the 1930s, it is likely that he would have found rationalizations for the Nazi rearmament and the undoing of the Versailles Treaty. On the other hand, he might have been sensitive to the fact that technological change had made Europe much closer to America than in 1917 and, for all its faults, the Kaiser's government did not approach the Nazis in venality.

The Japanese attack on Pearl Harbor and subsequent declaration of war by Hitler on the United States ended the career of Bob La Follette, Jr., as an isolationist. Along with Republican Senator Arthur Vandenberg of Michigan, he supported FDR and Truman on foreign affairs, thereafter. After the war, Bob Jr. led an ambitious reorganization of the Senate. Possibly due to demands of his office, possibly due to a lack of desire for hard political campaigning, the Senator devoted little energy to his 1946 re-election campaign.

In the Republican primary, La Follette was opposed by a little-known state judge from Appleton, Wisconsin, named Joseph R. McCarthy. The judge emphasized and exaggerated his war record, but in the end "Tail

---

[5]*La Follette's Weekly*, 17:65 (March 1925).

Gunner Joe" defeated Senator La Follette by 5,000 votes. In view of McCarthy's subsequent career, one of the great ironies of the campaign was that the challenger may have materially benefited from the hostility of Wisconsin Communists to La Follette, whom they considered no friend.

Bob, Jr. who had been the youngest United States Senator since Henry Clay, had done nothing in his life other than work for his father and be a Senator. He retired from politics completely at the age of 51. He was on the board of directors of Sears and Roebuck, was a Vice-President of the Sears Foundation, and served as a consultant to the United Fruit Company.

The ex-Senator began to experience some heart problems and according to some friends took his primary defeat by McCarthy very hard. Six years after his defeat, on February 24, 1953, he called his wife at work and told her to come home. When she arrived, she found him in the bathroom, where he had killed himself with a gunshot to the head. La Follette left no suicide note.[6]

The New York Times, a much more liberal newspaper than it had been in his father's time, characterized Bob, Jr. as "one of the most esteemed and useful members of the Senate. . . . " In a veiled reference to his pre-war isolationism, *The Times* observed, "If he had an inadequate perception of foreign relations, he had a keen understanding of domestic affairs. . . ."[7]

[6]*NYT*, February 25, 1953 1:3.

[7]*NYT*, February 26, 1953, 24:3.

Fola La Follette with Bob, Jr. and Phil

The La Follette statue in the U. S. Capitol

CHAPTER 9
Was He Right?

In an otherwise favorable review of Belle and Fola La Follette's biography, *Robert M. La Follette,* the noted historian, Henry Steele Commager, offered the following criticism:

> It never occurs to the authors to ask whether La Follette was right or wrong. By any tests whatsoever, La Follette's action was sincere, courageous and high-minded. By any tests the opposition to him was vindictive and absurd. But this does not mean that La Follette was right and Wilson was wrong in the great decision of April, 1917.[1]

Commager may have been asking too much of the Senator's daughter to make an objective judgment on the most controversial part of his career and, indeed, may have been asking the impossible of any writer. One thing that is striking about the issue of U.S. entry into World War I is how different it looks depending on whether you analyze it from the perspective of the late 1920s, from the perspective of the post-World War II era, or the post-Vietnam era.[2]

---

[1]*NYT,* December 20, 1953, VII, p. 7. As noted previously, the portions of the biography dealing with the Senator's career after 1910 were written by his daughter.

[2]A similar phenomenom is encountered by anyone doing a substantial amount of reading on the Reconstruction era. Conventional American history before the Civil Rights era of the 1960s treated Reconstruction as a mistake and depicted the whites who participated in it either as blindly vindictive (Thad Stevens) or opportunistic. The blacks involved were depicted as stooges of the corrupt white carpetbaggers. On the other hand, the white opponents of the Reconstruction governments were viewed as heroic. Accounts of the era written since the 1960s generally take a

During World War I, with the exception of some German-Americans, committed pacifists, and doctrinaire Socialists, La Follette was viewed by virtually everyone in the United States as wrong and blind to obvious venality of Imperial Germany. The Germans were viewed as having started the war by encouraging the Austrians to make war on Serbia. They were viewed as the aggressors in attacking neutral Belgium, and France—thus bringing a reluctant England into the war because of its moral obligations to the Belgians.

The Kaiser's government was similarly viewed as unnecessarily brutal in its treatment of Belgian civilians, its torpedoing of ocean liners, its initiation of gas warfare and the use of flame throwers, and the enslavement of citizens of occupied nations. Indeed, from the perspective of the war years, the best one could say for the La Follette point of view was that although he was correct in saying that the United States was not truly neutral, it could not have been—given the character of Imperial Germany.

Fifteen to twenty years later, Wilson and La Follette looked much different to many Americans. A sizeable number believed that U. S. entry into World War I was a mistake. The President had promised a war to end all wars. He promised a new system of international relations that would ensure justice and peaceful resolution of international conflict. After the passage of a decade and a half, it was difficult to see any positive result from the war. Europe was more unstable than it had been before. The conflict had produced Fascism, Nazism, and Communism, which only exacerbated the deep-seated national rivalries that predated the war. Small wonder it was that most Americans felt that Europe should be left to stew in its own juice.

During and after World War II, perceptions of the first global conflict changed again. Whatever justice had supported Germany's demands for revision of the Versailles Treaty, the unprecedented crimes committed during the Second World War suggested that if we were right to fight the Germans in the 1940s, we must also have been right to fight them in 1917.

---

completely contrary view.

Indeed, to many it seemed that what the second war proved was that we were too lenient in dealing with Germany after the first.

As the Second World War was the prism through which one generation viewed the world, so Vietnam became the prism through which much of the next generation views it. What Vietnam suggested was that Americans could rarely understand conditions abroad well enough to rationally influence the course of events in other countries, or disputes between two foreign contestants. The difference in the life experience between the two generations is exemplified by this author and his uncle. My uncle took part in pacifist demonstrations in college in the late 1920s but found himself, as an American infantryman, taking part in the assault on the German fortifications at Metz in November 1944. In retrospect, he viewed his collegiate activities as naive.

The author, raised on the lore of World War II and the dangers of appeasement, initially accepted the government's rationale for intervention in Vietnam uncritically. The 1968 Tet offensive proved as disillusioning to me as the rise of Hitler must have been to my uncle. My service as an army noncombatant in Saigon in 1970 is a source of ambivalence, not as military service was for my uncle, a source of unrestrained pride.

There is a strong link between the opposition to the Vietnam War and Senator La Follette's stand in 1917. Indeed, there is a direct connection in the person of Ernest Gruening, one of the two U. S. Senators who had the courage to vote against President Johnson's request for authority to bomb North Vietnam in retaliation for the alleged attack on U. S. ships in the Gulf of Tonkin. As noted previously, Gruening was the publicity manager for Senator La Follette's Presidential campaign in 1924.

Nevertheless, just as Senator La Follette's courage does not necessarily make him right, neither does the fact that Senator Gruening was right in 1964 (if he was in fact correct) mean that La Follette was right in 1917. However, in judging La Follette's place in history, the thing for which one must give him unqualified credit is that he refused to be bullied by Wilson or the prevailing public mood. He insisted on a dispassionate and rational examination of the reasons for which America proposed to enter the European war. La Follette was clearly correct in arguing that the United States had failed to assert its neutrality in an evenhanded

163

manner with respect to England and Germany. The American public should have been made aware of this fact—which it would not have been but for La Follette.

The Senator was also correct that the United States and certain business interests in the United States had a huge financial interest in an Allied victory. However, I would fault the Senator for attributing purely financial motives to everyone clamoring for intervention on the Allied side. There certainly were plenty of altruists among those calling for aid to France and Britain.

La Follette may also have been correct in arguing that by entering the war on the Allied side, America was relinquishing any chance it had of establishing a post-war world predicated on justice and likely to preserve the peace. The course of events after the war—the reparations, the unilateral assessment of war guilt, the creation of political and economic insecurity in Weimar Germany, and the subsequent rise of Hitler—confirmed the dire predictions made by La Follette between 1917 and 1920.

On the other hand, the Senator can be faulted for excessive evenhandedness. For every German delict, the Senator would come up with an English one, for example, the subjugation of India and Ireland and the secret inducements offered Italy to enter the war. A good argument can be made that the transgressions of the Germans were of a different order than those of France and England (although Czarist Russia was a tougher ally to defend), and that these differences justified the lack of evenhandedness in U.S. policy towards the belligerents.

During World War I, England was portrayed in America as a reluctant participant in the war. The British were viewed as having been forced to fight by pure idealism and national honor when Germany violated neutral Belgium. Revisionist historians in the late 1920s and 1930s portrayed the English differently. The British were viewed as opportunists, waiting to destroy their most threatening commercial competitor.

When Germany, faced with extinction by the Russian-French alliance, attacked France through Belgium as a matter of military necessity, England, some argued, sanctimoniously found a convenient excuse for doing what it wished to do all along. It is clearly correct that once France was at war, most of the English cabinet, including Prime Minister Asquith, Foreign Secretary Grey, and First Lord of the Admiralty Winston Churchill wanted to go to war even if the Germans did not attack Belgium. Britain's helping itself to German East Africa, after the conflict, is often cited as an example of the real motives behind its entry into the war.

The revisionist view emphasized the more indirect causes of the war, as opposed to the events of July 1914, in assessing responsibility for the war. The less one focuses on the Austrian ultimatum to Serbia and German complicity in Austrian belligerence, the easier it becomes to be sympathetic to the Kaiser. If one views the system of alliances, commercial competition, and imperialistic ventures as more important than the events immediately preceding the war, Germany appears hardly more responsible for the conflict than the Allies.

Whatever grievances the French had from 1870, it is not difficult to find fault with their entering into an alliance with Czarist Russia, the most reactionary regime in Europe. Given the obvious danger to German security in the event of a concurrent war with Russia and France, it becomes harder to take moral umbrage to the von Schlieffen plan, or the Kaiser's desire to assure the preservation of Austria-Hungary. Given the Germans' well-founded fears of the Franco-Russian alliance, the English insistence on the sanctity of Belgian neutrality, guaranteed by the European powers in 1839 when conditions were much different, can be viewed far less sympathetically. If England was that concerned with Belgium, should not it have pressured France to renounce or modify its treaty obligations with Russia.

On balance, this author thinks Senator La Follette was wrong in equating the war guilt of Germany, France, and England. Germany legitimately bears the lions' share of the responsibility for the outbreak of World War I. For all of its cries of victimization at Versailles, it was Germany which created the festering animus of France by annexing the French provinces of Alsace and Lorraine in 1870 and imposing war reparations on the French after the fall of Napoleon III.

165

Second, Kaiser Wilhelm bears much responsibility for the war in insisting on a naval arms race with England. Naval supremacy was not necessary for German security but was essential to the British. The Kaiser managed to overcome England's historic antipathy towards France, a nation with which the English barely avoided war in 1898 (the Fashoda incident in Africa). Had Wilhelm not challenged British naval supremacy, possibly England would have been responsive to the argument that the invasion of Belgium was a matter of self-defense.

Thirdly, although the precondition for World War I was the existence of the deep-seated national rivalries between France and Germany, and England and Germany, warfare could have been avoided if Austria, with Germany's encouragement, had not insisted on making war on Serbia in July 1914. The German government, much of which assumed that war was inevitable and preferred it sooner to later, did little to restrain Austria, or defuse the situation. While the German strategic plans made much sense militarily, one must fault Germany for not devising an alternative which might have localized or minimized the conflict (although the same can be said of Russia). The von Schlieffen plan became the tail that wagged the dog. Without any alternative, virtually any confrontation with Russia was virtually guaranteed to require war with England and France.[3]

Where Senator La Follette was clearly right was in predicting that by entering the war on the Allied side, we were greatly limiting our ability to fashion the post-war peace. Wilson's belief that the United States was going to be able to get the Allies to accept a post-war settlement along the lines of his Fourteen Points was incredibly naive. Given the Allies' lack of interest in a negotiated peace before America entered the war, Wilson should have anticipated that the Allies would insist on the fruits of victory, if they emerged victorious—even with our help.

---

[3] From the German standpoint, it was the lack of flexibility on the part of Russia that led to a world war instead of a localized conflict. Had Russia not ordered a general mobilization of its forces in response to the Austrian declaration of war on Serbia, the argument goes, the Kaiser could and would have avoided committing himself to a general war.

166

It should have been no surprise that the English and the French, who lost an entire generation in the muck of the Western front, were in no mood to listen to platitudes from an ally whose human investment in the war was minuscule in comparison to theirs. Even without Clemenceau's inbred hatred for everything German, no reasonable person should have expected the French, given their historical animosity towards Germany, their manpower losses, and the ruin of part of their territory, to be receptive to an appeal for leniency. Whether or not La Follette was correct in arguing that the United States should have remained neutral in April 1917, he certainly was correct in warning Americans of the pitfalls of tying ourselves so closely to the British and the French.

It is difficult to say that La Follette's proposals for pressure by the neutral nations in concert could have produced a settlement to the war. Nevertheless, one can argue that had the U.S. merely used force to protect its ships, similar to what was proposed in the Armed Ship bill, and continued to press for a negotiated settlement rather than send troops to Europe, that America's interests would have been better served.

The collapse of Russia and the withdrawal from the war by the Bolsheviks released a sufficient number of German troops from the East that the Allies could never have won the war without American troops. Had the United States simply helped keep the sealanes to England open, and thereby contributed indirectly to the British blockade of Germany, it appears that a German victory in the west was unlikely. Once the Germans had played the submarine card and found it wanting, they might have been more agreeable to a negotiated settlement of the war.

Conversely, had England and France known that there was no prospect for getting millions of American troops into action, they may also have been more likely to compromise. Had the Kaiser, or a relative, stayed on the German throne, the subsequent history of Europe may have been less tragic. A German government with Wilhelm as the nominal head of state could not have been any less stable or more subservient to the military than the Weimar Republic. Looking backwards in April 1945, Winston Churchill observed, "[I]f [the Allies] had allowed a Hohenzollern, a Wittelsbach, and a Habsburg to return to their thrones, there would have been no Hitler."[4] It is quite possible that the power of the Reichstag would have grown and that the Kaiser's power after the war would have much more that of a constitutional monarch.[5]

The counterargument is that the problem with Allied post-war policy was not that it was too harsh, but that it was not harsh enough. Marshall Ferdinand Foch passionately urged permanent Allied occupation of Germany west of the Rhine—rather than reliance on German good will to prevent a recurrence of the war. Similarly many lay blame for the Second World War on the American isolationists, who undermined President Wilson's attempt to establish a collective security system in the form of the League of Nations. The difficulty with this point of view is that even with the League, maintaining a harsh peace would have depended on the continued willingness of the Allies to use force to meet any German attempt to redress what it believed to be the injustice of the post-war settlement.

By the 1930s, when Hitler railed against the Versailles Treaty, many in the West saw enough merit in his arguments that they were not instantaneously willing to commence another war. Even without a League of Nations, France and England, or even France alone could have attacked Germany before it rearmed—if public opinion in those countries would have tolerated such action. The fact that this was not so until 1939 would have been true even if the United States had joined the League of Nations.

Ironic it is that two of the men most responsible for the outcome of the Versailles conference had first-hand experiences that should have served as a warning as to how difficult it would be to maintain its terms. Georges Clemenceau, the 78-year-old French prime minister, spent several

---

[4]Gilbert, *Churchill*, p. 837.

[5]The obvious parallel is the decision to keep Hirohito on the Japanese throne after World War II, which contributed greatly to his nation's acceptance of the American-imposed democracy. Finding the right Hohenzollern may have been tricky as several of the Kaiser's sons turned out to be ardent Nazis and may have been just as bellicose as their father. However, Prince Louis Ferdinand, son of the Crown Prince Wilhelm, was deemed sufficiently anti-Nazi to be considered as a potential head of state by the conspirators who tried to kill Hitler in 1944.

years in America after the Civil War as a newspaper reporter, and covered the impeachment trial of Andrew Johnson. Whether he realized it or not, he witnessed a sequence of events which should have given him some cause for reflection as to the likely consequences of his position at Versailles. Woodrow Wilson, who spent his childhood in the wartime Confederacy, and then in the reconstructed South, also had reason to ponder these events.

After defeating the Confederates militarily, the victorious North tried first to subjugate the vanquished permanently. They attempted to destroy the economic and political power of the landholding aristocracy and Southern military caste. The federal government tried for a few years to fundamentally change the relationship of blacks and whites in the South and then lost interest. The white Southerners initially were cowed by the federal army occupation and the Freedman's Bureau. They nursed their desire for revenge until it became evident that the Northerners no longer had the stomach for renewed warfare. The whites rearmed and through violence and intimidation reclaimed their homeland.

President Hayes in agreeing to the final withdrawal of federal troops in 1877 was in a situation similar to that of Chamberlain and Daladier in 1938. The reality he faced was that it was much more important to the Southern whites, as it was to the Germans in 1938, to return to pre-war conditions than it was to the victors to preserve the immediate post-war order. As Hitler was ready to fight in 1938 and England and France were not, so Wade Hampton and his followers were ready to fight for white rule in South Carolina in 1877, while the federal government was no longer willing to fight to maintain reconstruction.

In the final analysis, as the Civil War analogy shows, Senator La Follette was correct in his opposition to the Versailles Treaty—which, as he predicted, only increased the possibilities of another war. What is more difficult to say is whether it would have been possible for the United States to have assured an Allied victory and then to have used the enormous economic leverage it enjoyed to dictate a productive post-war settlement, not only on the Germans, but also on the English and French.

169

CHAPTER 10

Wilson, Theodore Roosevelt, and La Follette

The career of Robert M. La Follette, Sr., is closely intertwined with that of Theodore Roosevelt and Woodrow Wilson, the two most important figures in American history during the first quarter of the twentieth century. Both are conventionally regarded as great or near-great Presidents. The three men represented three conflicting schools of thought with regard to American intervention in World War I. Roosevelt, by early 1915, felt that America had to enter the war on the side of the Allies in order to preserve its national honor.

Wilson, although sympathetic with the Allies from the outset of the war, either felt that intervention was unwarranted, unnecessary, or politically unwise—until the Germans resumed unrestricted submarine warfare in 1917. La Follette, of course, was truly neutral and believed American participation in the war was never justified or wise. As World War I was the most important issue any of these men addressed during their careers, any judgment of their respective places in history should include comparative assessment of their positions. If one of these men was right, the other two were certainly wrong.

As to Theodore Roosevelt, one must start by giving him credit for having the courage of his convictions. As in the Spanish-American War, he was not an "arm-chair jingo" and had no intention of having others fight the war while he and his sons stayed at home. TR did not fight in France only because President Wilson wouldn't let him. All four of his sons fought; Ted, Jr., and Archie were wounded, and his youngest boy, Quentin, died in aerial combat.

If the Germans or their government were so inherently evil and/or a German victory would have been so threatening to the United States as Theodore Roosevelt believed, he was clearly right in arguing that we

171

should have declared war in May 1915, when the *Lusitania* sank, if not earlier. Roosevelt and Wilson could not both have been right. Wilson, it seems, would not have entered the war but for the U-boats. Had the Germans been a little more patient, they may not have needed to reinstitute submarine warfare and could have avoided war with the United States. The collapse of Russia may have allowed them to achieve victory or at least a stalemate in which the Kaiser would have retained control of Belgium and northeastern France.

In judging the Roosevelt view, one must take into account the fact that Theodore Roosevelt was a man who loved war and regarded it as the area for the greatest achievements of the human race. As Assistant Secretary of the Navy in 1897, TR told the Naval War College that "no triumph of peace is quite as great as the supreme triumph of war."[1] Roosevelt was consistent in this view throughout his career and rarely encountered an opportunity to involve the United States in warfare that he found wanting. Whether it was fighting the Spanish in Cuba, the Spanish in the Philippines, the Filipino nationalists, or the Kaiser, TR was all for it. Thus, it's hard to separate a good war from a bad war through the eyes of Theodore Roosevelt, because he hardly ever judged any war to be the wrong one—except possibly the war between Japan and Russia.

If, on the other hand, the Germans were not so evil or threatening that we were not compelled to help the Allies win, Roosevelt was wrong and La Follette was right. Indeed, it is most difficult logically to defend Wilson because if La Follette was wrong; the President was not necessarily right. If as La Follette believed there was nothing to choose from between the Allies and the Central Powers, Wilson should have followed a course of strict neutrality—which he did not. If, on the other hand, Roosevelt was right, he should never have espoused neutrality and should have been in the Allies' corner certainly by May 1915.

Had the Germans been confronted by millions of American troops in 1916, rather than 1918, the war may have been much shorter, less costly, and less disruptive for the future. Indeed, in 1916 the Americans would have arrived on the Western front while the Germans still had their hands

---

[1]Morris, *The Rise of Theodore Roosevelt*, p. 569.

full in the East, contrary to the situation in 1918. If Wilson was able to sell the war to the American people in 1917 with only a few American casualties at sea, he could have done so immediately after the sinking of the *Lusitania*.

What is hardest to justify is the proposition that German venality did not warrant American intervention before 1917, but did so afterwards when our complicity in the British naval blockade led the Kaiser to resort to submarine warfare to break the stalemate on the Western front. It is true that until February 1, 1917, Wilson had deluded himself into believing that he could mediate an end to the war. The resumption of submarine warfare ended this misconception. It is also true that psychologically, the resumption of U-boat warfare and the Zimmermann telegram cried out for some sort of action by the U.S. government. It would have been impossible, as Senator La Follette advocated, to announce that our less-than-neutral policy had been mistaken and that we would begin to enforce our rights against both sides. Nevertheless it is difficult to give Wilson a lot of credit for backing himself into a corner where we would be forced into the war anytime Germany decided that the advantages of the submarine outweighed the dangers of American intervention.

Roosevelt was absolved of responsibility for the post-war settlement by his death in January 1919. However, there is no doubt that had he lived, he, and not his close friend, Henry Cabot Lodge, would have been Wilson's primary adversary with regard to the League of Nations. TR, at his death, was the odds-on favorite to be the Republican Presidential candidate in 1920 (he was only 60). There is no way he would have allowed Wilson, who also wanted a third term, to run as the man who won the peace, as well as the war.

Wilson is generally considered a great President for: 1) keeping us out of war until 1917; 2) getting us into the war; 3) his Fourteen Points speech which he repudiated by virtually everything he did at Versailles; and 4) the League of Nations. Yet in the final analysis his reputation rises and falls on the premise that he had a realistic plan that would have prevented the Second World War—if Americans had only been less short-sighted.

At Versailles, Wilson discovered that structuring the post-war world was not going to be nearly as easy as it seemed. He took an abstract concept, the League of Nations, and elevated it to the paramount issue of the conference. Realizing that he had no solution to the immediate problems of the day, he held up the League as a panacea for all the world's problems.

Wilson led off the conference by getting Clemenceau to agree to the formation of the League. Then Clemenceau named his price—American acquiescence to French demands for war reparations, a clause in the treaty attributing all responsibility for the war to Germany, and other measures that from the outset created outrage throughout Germany and made the Weimar Republic vulnerable to right-wing intrigue. Bob La Follette, Jr., at the end of World War II, made the following observations on the President's performance at Versailles:

> Because the United States had failed to exact a commitment to specific democratic peace terms from the European Allies when our bargaining power was prodigious, President Wilson was driven into surrendering principle after principle during the actual process of formulating the peace treaty at Versailles. The President mistakenly believed that a league of nations could subsequently right the injustices of the Versailles Treaty. . . . Many tragic consequences followed President Wilson's absorption in securing world organization at the expense of a just peace. . . . The terms of the Versailles Treaty doomed the League from the beginning. . . .[2]

The President, a former political science professor, did nothing to maximize the chances that the U.S. Senate would ratify the treaty. Having lost control of the Congress in 1918 to the Republicans, Wilson was completely out-of-touch with reality in assuming that he could have forced the treaty through the Senate by going directly to the people.

---

[2]*Congressional Record*, Vol. 91, pt. 4 (May 31, 1945), pp. 5318-9.

However, in judging Woodrow Wilson, the most important thing to realize is that even if the United States had entered the League in 1921, there was no guarantee that the League would have used force to uphold the Versailles Treaty or preserve the peace in the 1930s. Action by the League would still have required willingness by France, England, and the United States to send troops to Germany to prevent rearmament, remilitarization of the Rhineland, the Anschluss of Austria, the annexation of the Sudetenland, etc. If even France was unwilling to go to war at these various junctures in Hitler's unravelling of the Versailles Treaty, it is certain that the United States, even if it had joined the League, would have been unwilling to commit troops to enforce the peace terms of 1919. League or no League, England and France could not have compelled the United States to send troops to Europe against its will.

In trading the practical concerns of building a stable, peaceable Europe for the abstraction of the League of Nations, Wilson probably did more lasting damage than any man who has held the office of President of the United States. This extremely low assessment of Woodrow Wilson, although inconsistent with the conventional view, is shared by others. Among his detractors are several historians cited in an article entitled "Overrated and Underrated Americans" which appeared in the July-August 1988 issue of *American Heritage*.

For this article a number of historians and journalists picked the American historical figure they considered most overrated and the one they regarded to be the most underrated. Several Americans icons were viewed as most overrated by several of the contributors, and some who were considered most overrated by one person were viewed as the most underrated by another. However, the figures receiving the harshest treatment were Wilson, Theodore Roosevelt, Thomas Jefferson, John F. Kennedy, and Ronald Reagan. Wallace Stegner, author of the novel *Angle of Repose* rated Wilson as the most underrated. The less flattering assessments were as follows:

175

Peter Andrews, contributing editor, *American Heritage*:

> Most overrated: Woodrow Wilson in a walk. Never has the peril of having a truly good man in the White House been more clearly demonstrated. His dictation of peace terms at Versailles was one of the seminal blunders of his century, and his overweening vanity and his sense of self-righteousness did as much to sabotage the League of Nations as anything Henry Cabot Lodge thought of.

Richard Crunden, Professor of History, University of Texas, Austin:

> Most overrated: Woodrow Wilson. He was a provincial who appeared cosmopolitan, an academic who could not tolerate the free play of ideas or the minds of any women, and a world leader whose obsessions befouled human discourse and contributed materially to the chaos of the succeeding decades.

John Lukacs, Professor of History, Chestnut Hill College:

> Most Overrated: Woodrow Wilson. A man of superficial ideas but no real principles, an academic politician ignorant of the world; the proponent of an abstract internationalism that was adopted by Republicans as well as Democrats—in sum, the founding father of our globalist predicaments.

I would go so far as to question Mr. Andrews' characterization of President Wilson as a "truly good man." He imposed racial segregation in government offices, where it had never existed before—after courting black votes in 1912. No American President tolerated such wide-spread suppression of civil liberties as the academic from Princeton. He was quoted as bemoaning the fate of civil liberties at the outbreak of the war but did nothing to curb the violence done to them by his Postmaster General, Arthur Burleson, and his Attorney General, A. Mitchell Palmer.

176

His insistence on keeping Eugene V. Debs in prison is also hard to square with his essential goodness. Debs—if nothing else—was a sincere man of principle, and Wilson's refusal to commute his sentence in 1920 and 1921 can only be characterized as cruel. How odd it is that the much-villified Warren G. Harding was able to find some compassion for Debs, while Wilson was not. Although it's true that Wilson's judgment may have been affected by his stroke—his acquisence in the suppression of non-conforming ideas by Postmaster Burleson occurred before his illness.

Everyone is smarter with the benefit of hindsight, but historical figures are normally judged by the luck they experienced in dealing with the confusing situations with which they were confronted. Wilson, it seems to me, deserves to be judged a complete failure. While it is impossible to say what would have transpired had the nation listened to Bob La Follette between 1915 and 1925, I think that it is most likely that the subsequent history of the world would have been far less tragic. On this basis alone, I think Robert Marion La Follette was the greatest American of the first quarter of the the twentieth century.

CHAPTER 11
Author's Note

I am a 1967 graduate of Miami University, Oxford, Ohio. Ironically, in my senior year, I was awarded the Atlee Pomerene Award for scholastic excellence by the Government Department.[1] In 1972, I graduated from the Harvard Law School, after serving two years as a draftee in the United States Army. One of those years was spent working for the U. S. Army Procurement Agency in Saigon, South Vietnam. My professional career has been spent in the law, but I consider myself a serious amateur historian. My interest in Robert La Follette and his opposition to America's involvement in the First World War arose from an intensive study of American history which I began in 1982. I started with the Civil War and the events leading up to it and have found our nation's past to be "a seamless web."

One of the things that has intrigued me is that for certain periods of our history, particularly the Civil War, World War II, and Vietnam, there is an inexhaustable amount of material, while for much of the rest of our history there is very little in the way of books for the general reader. A large public library will have shelves and shelves of books on the Civil War, the Second World War, and Vietnam, and only a few books on the Spanish-American War, World War I, the Korean Conflict and those relatively quiet periods such as 1865 to 1898 and the first quarter of the twentieth century.

---

[1]In researching this book, I consulted a biographical directory of the members of the U. S. Congress and discovered, coincidentally, that the most authoritative source on the career of Atlee Pomerene is the doctoral thesis of Dr. Philip R. Shriver, who happened to be President of Miami University during my undergraduate days. This led me to exchange letters with Dr. Shriver, now President Emeritus, whom I did not know personally as a student.

179

I have previously written two historical books. The first, *The Most Famous Soldier in America: Nelson A. Miles, 1839–1925,* is a biography of one of the Civil War's "boy generals" whose career continued into some of the lesser-known epochs; the Indian Wars, the Spanish War and the Philippine Insurrection. My second book, *Heroes, Martyrs, and Survivors of the Civil War,* is a collection of biographical sketches of Civil War figures. By following some of the survivors after the war, I taught myself quite a bit about the Reconstruction period, the reaction to Reconstruction, and the rest of late nineteenth-century American history.

Tracing such Civil War veterans as President McKinley, General Miles, and General Joseph Wheeler (the former Confederate Major-General who commanded the U. S. Cavalry in Cuba) to the Spanish-American War led me to William Jennings Bryan and the opposition to U. S. military intervention in the Philippines between 1898 and 1902. My interest in Bryan led me to his resignation as Secretary of State in 1915 and piqued my curiosity about the First World War. I was curious whether we had gone to war, as Bryan warned after the *Lusitania* sinking, to protect the right of a small number of Americans to sail to Europe on British ships.

As I began to read, I was quite astonished about how little I really knew about why we went to war in 1917. I recalled from school that we had gone to war to preserve freedom of the seas. However, as Bryan phrased it, that seemed an awfully inadequate reason to fight.

Bryan's role as an opponent of U. S. policy with regards to the conflict ended with the Congressional declaration of war in April 1917. From that point on, it is La Follette, who almost alone among American politicans, continued to publicly ask troubling questions about our involvement. Even George Norris, who was very outspoken in the Senatorial debate on the war resolution kept his mouth shut once war was declared.

Prior to researching this book, all I knew about Bob La Follette was that he was a leader of the Progressive movement in the early part of the twentieth century. Although, I knew he was a "great man," I confess that much of what the Progressive movement was about was not that interesting to me. The direct primary and the direct election of Senators were important measures, but it seems to me that the influence of money is even more important in American politics today than it was in La

180

Follette's time. Indeed, the increased democratization of the political process has made television the primary mechanism of reaching the people. In turn, the cost of television time has made it virtually impossible for one to campaign for anything without substantial financial support from some coalition of special interest groups.

La Follette's stand against the war, however, is a little-known episode in American history that warrants constant retelling. The mass hysteria that accompanied American entry into World War I should provoke somber reflection whenever military intervention is being considered abroad. Since 1917, those Americans who have had the audacity to question subsequent U. S. military action have not received a much more sympathetic hearing than did La Follette. Even with regard to the recent Persian Gulf War, the pressure to fall in line with those advocating the use of force was intense.

In some ways, writing this book has been a bit distressing. My father idolized Franklin D. Roosevelt and Woodrow Wilson. He taught me that FDR saved America and the world from Hitler while the Midwest isolationists, Borah, Nye, and Wheeler, made it as difficult as possible for him to do so.

Discovering Woodrow Wilson's feet of clay has not been a happy experience. I also found it difficult to accept the fact that Germany had many legitimate grievances both with regard to World War I and the Peace of Versailles. As a Jew looking at these events with the perspective of the Holocaust, it is not easy to admit that Hitler's rise to power was in part due to what are at least half-truths. Nevertheless, nothing can excuse the scapegoating the vast majority of Germans participated in or at least tolerated.

My fascination with history has always been in part a search for heroes. In our nation's history, I have found a number. Although, I regard such American icons as Wilson and Theodore Roosevelt to be completely undeserving of their historical reputations, I have found figures such as Lincoln and Grant to be every bit as heroic as I was taught in elementary school. I have also discovered lesser-known figures, such as Carl Schurz, worthy of veneration. If for no other reason this project was worth

181

completing for acquainting me with another bona fide American hero, Robert M. La Follette.

Selected Bibliography

UNPUBLISHED WORKS

The La Follette Family Papers, Library of Congress
National Archives documents on the proceedings of the Senate
    Committee on Privileges and Elections

NEWSPAPERS AND MAGAZINES

American Heritage
Cincinnati Enquirer
Cincinnati Post
Cincinnati Times-Star
Congressional Record
Current History
Current Opinion
Everybody's Magazine
La Follette's
Literary Digest
Milwaukee Journal
Milwaukee Sentinel
The Nation
The New Republic
New York Evening Post
The New York Times
New York Tribune
New York World
North American Review
The Outlook
Time
The Washington Post

Washington Star
Wisconsin State Journal
World's Work

BOOKS

Alexander, Holmes, *The Famous Five,* 1958.
Arnett, Alex Mathews, *Claude Kitchen and the Wilson War Policies,* 1937.
Ashhurst, Henry F., *A Many Colored Toga,* 1962.
Asinof, Eliot, *1919: America's Loss of Innocence,* 1990.
Bailey, Thomas A., *Woodrow Wilson and the Great Betrayal,* 1945.
Bailey, Thomas A., *Woodrow Wilson and the Lost Peace,* 1944.
Beaver, Dan, *Buckeye Crusader* [biography of Herbert Bigelow], 1957.
Bernstorff, Count Johann von, *Memoirs,* 1936.
Bernstorff, Count Johann von, *My Three Years in America,* 1920.
Burgchardt, Carl R., *Robert M. La Follette, Sr.: The Voice of Conscience,* 1992.
Chambers, John Whiteclay, *To Raise an Army: The Draft Comes to America,* 1987.
Cohen, Warren I., *The American Revisionist: The Lessons of Intervention in World War I,* 1967.
Cole, Wayne S., *America First: The Battle Against Intervention, 1940-1941,* 1971.
Darrow, Clarence, *Autobiography.*
Davidson, Eugene, *The Making of Adolf Hitler: The Birth and Rise of Nazism,* 1977.
Dorapalen, Andreas, *Hindenberg and the Weimar Republic,* 1964.
Dornberg, John, *Munich 1923: The Story of Hitler's First Grab for Power,* 1982.
Ellis, Edward Robb, *Echoes of Distant Thunder: Life in the United States 1914-1918,* 1975.
Ferrell, Robert H., *Woodrow Wilson and World War I,* 1985.
Friedrich, Otto, *Before the Deluge: A Portrait of Berlin in the 1920s,* 1972.

Gardner, Joseph L., *Departing Glory: Theodore Roosevelt as Ex-President,* 1973.

Garraty, John A., *Henry Cabot Lodge,* 1953.

Gilbert, Martin, *Churchill: A Life,* 1991.

Ginger, Ray, *The Bending Cross* [biography of Eugene V. Debs], 1947.

Goodspeed, D. J., *Ludendorff: Genius of World War I,* 1966.

Harbaugh, William, *Lawyer's Lawyer: The Life of John W. Davis,* 1973.

Heckscher, August, *Woodrow Wilson,* 1991.

Holmes, William F., *The White Chief: James Kimble Vardaman,* 1970.

Jackson, J. Hampden, *Clemenceau and the Third Republic,* 1948.

Joll, James, *The Origins of the First World War,* 1983.

Kennedy, David M., *Over Here,* 1980.

Kitchen, Martin, *The Silent Dictatorship,* 1976.

Koenig, Louis W., *Bryan,* 1971.

La Follette, Belle Case and Fola, *Robert M. La Follette* (2 volumes), 1953.

La Follette, Robert M., *Autobiography,* 1913.

Lafore, Laurence, *The Long Fuse,* 1965.

Lindbergh, Charles, *The Wartime Journals of Charles A. Lindbergh,* 1970..

Lowitt, Richard, *George W. Norris: The Triumph of a Progressive, 1933-1944,* 1978

Luebke, Frederick C., *Bonds of Loyalty: German Americans and World War I,* 1974.

Maddox, Robert James, *William E. Borah and American Foreign Policy,* 1969.

Maney, Patrick J. *"Young Bob" La Follette: A biography of Robert M. La Follette, Jr., 1895-1953,* 1978.

Margulies, Herbert F., *Senator Lenroot of Wisconsin: A Political Biography,* 1977.

Mee, Charles L., Jr., *The End of Order: Versailles, 1919,* 1980.

Middleton, George, *These Things Are Mine,* 1947.

Millis, Walter, *The Road to War,* 1935.

Mock, James R., *Censorship 1917,* 1941.

185

Moore, Howard, *Plowing My Own Furrow* [a COs experience in World War I], 1985.
Morison, Etling (ed.), *The Letters of Theodore Roosevelt,* volumes 7 and 8, 1954.
Nearing, Scott, *The Making of a Radical,* 1972.
Nelson, Keith, *Victors Divided: America and the Allies in Germany, 1918-1923,* 1975.
Neuberger, Richard L., and Kahn, Stephen B., *Integrity: The Life of George W. Norris* [co-author Neuberger was later a Senator from Oregon], 1937.
Noggle, Paul, *Teapot Dome: Oil and Politics in the 1920s,* 1962.
Norris, George W., *Fighting Liberal: The Autobiography of George W. Norris,* 1945.
Palmer, Alan, *Bismarck,* 1976.
Palmer, Alan, *The Kaiser: Warlord of the Second Reich,* 1978.
Panichas, George (ed.), *Promise of Greatness: The War of 1914-1918,* 1968.
Parkinson, Roger, *Tormented Warrior: Ludendorff and the Supreme Command,* 1978.
Rowland, Peter, *David Lloyd George,* 1975.
Ryley, Thomas W., *A Little Group of Willful Men* [an excellent, short, and very readable account of the filibuster over the Armed Ship Bill], 1975.
Selections from the Correspondence of Theodore Roosevelt and Henry Cabot Lodge, 1884-1918, vol. 2, 1925.
Steffens, Lincoln, *Autobiography,* 1931.
Stokesbury, James L., *A Short History of World War I,* 1981.
Sullivan, Mark, *Our Times,* volumes 4, 5, and 6.
Thelen, David P., *Robert La Follette and the Insurgent Spirit,* 1976.
Toland, John, *Adolf Hitler.*
Truman, Harry S., *The Buck Stops Here* [includes HST's very favorable assessment of his commander-in-chief, Woodrow Wilson], 1989.
Tuchman, Barbara, *The Guns of August,* 1962.
Tuchman, Barbara, *The Zimmerman Telegram,* 1958.
Walworth, Arthur, *Woodrow Wilson,* 1974.

Watt, Richard, *Dare Call It Treason* [one of the most interesting books
   for the general reader on any aspect of World War I—about French
   politics during the war], 1963.
Watt, Richard M., *The Kings Depart: The Tragedy of Germany;
   Versailles and the German Revolution,* 1968.
Wheeler, Burton K. and Healy, Paul F., *Yankee from the West,* 1962.
White, William Allen, *The Citizen's Business,* 1924.
Williams, Wythe, *The Tiger of France: Conversations with Clemenceau,*
   1949.
Young, Donald (editor), *Adventures in Politics: The Memoirs of Philip La
   Follette,* 1970.

Index

AMCHAN PUBLICATIONS
P.O. BOX 3648
ALEXANDRIA, VIRGINIA 22302

HEROES, MARTYRS, AND SURVIVORS OF THE CIVIL WAR
by Arthur J. Amchan

ISBN 0-9617132-2-4 $18.95 plus $1.00 shipping, illustrated, with index.

Biographical sketches of twenty-two notable Civil War-era figures. *The Flower of New England*: Oliver Wendell Holmes, Jr., Paul Joseph Revere, Robert Gould Shaw (the protagonist of the movie *Glory*), Charles Russell Lowell, Jr., Josephine Shaw Lowell, Henry L. Abbott, and Thomas Wentworth Higginson, the abolitionist minister who financed John Brown and commanded a regiment of freed slaves during the war; *From the Battlefield to the Presidency*: Ulysses S. Grant, Rutherford B. Hayes, James A. Garfield, Benjamin Harrison, and William McKinley; *the Other Side:* Robert E. Lee, Nathan Bedford Forrest, Wade Hampton, James Longstreet, and Joseph Wheeler; *Two Volunteers Who Became Professional Soldiers*: Nelson A. Miles and Arthur MacArthur; Plus Carl Schurz, the German revolutionary and Union general; Julius Peter Garesche, and Joseph Foraker, the U.S. Senator and Union veteran who confronted Theodore Roosevelt over his dismissal of 167 black soldiers from the U. S. Army in 1906.

"This series of eloquent biographical sketches links the military actions of the war with its broader social and cultural impact. *Heroes, Martyrs, and Survivors of the Civil War* should be on the shelves of every school library and public library as well as in the libraries of Civil War buffs."
— Professor James M. McPherson,
Author of *the Battle Cry of Freedom*

"Arthur Amchan has written two splendid books on the American Civil War. *Heroes, Martyrs, and Survivors of the Civil War* [and] *The Most Famous Soldier in America.* . . . Here is military biography at its best!"
— The Midwest Book Review

Continued on next page

THE MOST FAMOUS SOLDIER IN AMERICA: NELSON A. MILES, 1839–1925
by Arthur J. Amchan

ISBN 0-9617132-1-6 $14.95 plus $1.00 shipping, illustrated, with index.

A biography of Nelson A. Miles, a twenty-one-year-old clerk in a Boston crockery store who rose to Major-General in the Union Army. Virtually no individual in American history participated in as many famous historical events as General Miles and few have been as controversial. He was Jefferson Davis' jailer at Ft. Monroe in 1865-66 and placed the Confederate President in leg irons for several days.

One of the Army's most successful Indian fighters, Miles was instrumental in subjugating the Sioux after Custer's Last Stand and received the surrender of Chief Joseph of the Nez Perce and Geronimo. Commander of the Army's Division of the Missouri, Miles was very critical of his subordinates at Wounded Knee.

Commanding General of the Army from 1895-1903, Miles captured Puerto Rico during the Spanish-American War and crossed swords with Theodore Roosevelt over the President's conduct of the war in the Philippines.

Described by *The New York World* in 1903 as "the most distinguished American soldier now living," Miles was also described as "a perfect curse" by President Theodore Roosevelt a year earlier.

"A fascinating study of one of the most remarkable and controversial of that extraordinary breed of Americans—civilians at the outbreak of the Civil War who rose through the ranks of the Union Army to become outstanding professional commanders."
— Professor James M. McPherson
Author of *The Battle Cry of Freedom*

"A portrait that is well balanced . . . the only recent study of one of the great unsung American military figures. . . ."
— American Library Association *Booklist*

"It is ironic that everyone knows the name of Gen. George Custer, a flop at battling Indians, while the mention of Gen. Nelson A. Miles, possibly America's most successful Indian fighter, draws no recognition. Arthur Amchan tries to right the wrong with this excellent softcover biography of Miles."
— George Shestak, *The Omaha World Herald*

"This book should be read by anyone who is interested in the American military campaigns from 1860 to 1920. There are plenty of footnotes, but they are interesting, and the book is easy to read".
— J.R. Curtis, *True West*

ORDER FORM

Please send me:

HEROES, MARTYRS, AND SURVIVORS OF THE CIVIL WAR
_____copies X $18.95 each $_____

THE MOST FAMOUS SOLDIER IN AMERICA
_____copies X $14.95 each $_____

THE KAISER'S SENATOR
_____ copies X $14.95 each $_____

VA residents add 4 ½% sales tax. $_____
Less Discount (see below) $_____
Shipping $1 per book $_____

                              TOTAL ENCLOSED $_____

NAME_____

ADDRESS_____

_____ ZIP CODE_____

DISCOUNTS: For orders of:
·   5 or more books, deduct 10% from the price of the books
·   10 or more books, deduct 20% from the price of the books
·   20 or more books, deduct 30% from the price of the books

Mail Orders to:
    Amchan Publications
    P.O. Box 3648
    Alexandria, Virginia 22302

AMCHAN PUBLICATIONS
7010 Westbury Rd
McLean VA 22101
(703) 893 4717